MINERVA'S STEPCHILD

This Book Belongs To
Fatehia

HELEN FORRESTER

Minerva's Stepchild

To Fatehia,
Best wishes,
Helen Forrester

THE BODLEY HEAD (CANADA) LTD
TORONTO AND LONDON
In Association With
CLARKE IRWIN COMPANY LIMITED
TORONTO VANCOUVER

To my family and my friends
who helped me to remember

ISBN 0-370-30197-8
© 1979 by Jamunadevi Bhatia
Printed in Great Britain for
The Bodley Head (Canada) Ltd
335 Bay Street, Toronto
by Redwood Burn Ltd, Trowbridge
Set in Monotype Imprint 101
by Gloucester Typesetting Co. Ltd.
First published 1979

Chapter one

It had begun to rain and I was shivering, as I manoeuvered the squeaking Chariot over the road to the corner of Castle Street. Avril was red in the face with rage. She stormed at me because I would not take her out of the pram and let her walk amid the busy lunchtime crowd. At the other end of the pram, beneath the leaking hood, Baby Edward grizzled miserably for the same reason.

Since the October day was too cold for us to walk in the park, I had brought them into the city, thinking that it would be more sheltered and that we could amuse ourselves looking in the shop windows. And now we had wandered into the business district.

Pretty secretaries, rushing back from lunch, and smart businessmen, carrying umbrellas and brief cases, glanced impatiently at the intruding pram with two grubby urchins in noisy protest. It belonged away in the slums, like the tatterdemalion who pushed it.

I did not care. I was resigned to people staring at my long, wind-chapped, bare legs, at my toes sticking through a pair of old plimsolls, at an outgrown gym slip worn without a blouse, a ragged cardigan covering part of my nakedness.

Through the increasing rain, I pushed the pram

dreamily amongst them. In my mind I was not walking in black, depressing Liverpool; I was in the countryside and then in the fine, old southern town from which I had been unceremoniously plucked two years before. It was market day, and Father and I were looking at the horses brought in for sale. As we moved about, the ploughmen, the shepherds and the farmers would touch their forelocks to the distinguished-looking gentleman, strolling around with a little daughter in the uniform of a good private school.

'*Echo! Liverpool Echo.* Read all about it!' shouted a man in a cloth cap, thrusting a paper towards the hurrying throng. I blinked, and hurriedly swerved to avoid him.

Would we always have to stay in Liverpool, I wondered depressedly. Would we always be cold and hungry?

'Oh, shut up, Avril,' I scolded crossly, and stopped the pram while I tucked an old overcoat round Baby Edward's knees and then pushed the edges of it up over her lap. 'Look, love. See up there – on the top of the town hall. There's Minerva. She's looking at you.'

Avril turned her woebegone face upwards towards the dome I had pointed out.

'See,' I said. 'She's smiling at you. Hasn't she got a lovely golden face? But I think she's got smuts on her nose, just like you.' I touched Avril's damp, little nose with a playful finger, and she sniffed and stopped crying.

Baby Edward could not see what I had pointed out; but, when I touched his nose and laughed at him, he saw hope of a game and tried to reach forward to touch my hooked nose. Tiny fingers grasped at my horn-rimmed glasses. I backed away hastily before they fell off.

Laughing at each other, we continued along the street.

Many people thought it was Britannia who sat looking down at Liverpool, but Father had told me it was Minerva, the Goddess of Wisdom, Invention and Handicrafts. He assured me that she also took care of dramatic poets and actors.

There were plenty of craftsmen in Liverpool of whom she might have been proud, even some actors and a poet or two, but most of them queued at the Labour Exchanges, their abilities unused. They stood idly round the dock gates, where ships lay in every stage of decay. They hung around outside the gaily lit public houses. Her sailors, skilled men, sat hungry in their cold kitchens, while their despairing wives nagged and their children went barefoot.

Amongst the defeated men in the queues at the Labour Exchange, Father had stood for over two years. Ruined by the Depression and, in part, by his own extravagances, he had brought us back to his native city in the hope of finding work. But, in the Liverpool wet, he had seemed like a lost butterfly, with wings beaten useless by the rain. He had watched, helpless, as Mother struggled, without medical aid, to recuperate from a major operation and a mental breakdown. Though the wartime marriage had not been a happy one, her degeneration into a haggard virago must have broken his heart.

To look at his seven children was almost too much for him. We were a hungry, ragged and increasingly unruly crew, disoriented by our parents' disasters, seven small sparrows with our beaks open, loudly demanding to be fed.

Because Mother was at first so ill, I suddenly had thrust upon me, as the eldest child, the task of caring for her and for my brothers and sisters. The Public Assistance Committee gave Father forty-three shillings a week, out of which we paid twenty-seven shillings a week for three unheated attic rooms. The remaining sixteen shillings had to cover every need of nine people; and for a time it seemed certain that Baby Edward would die for lack of milk, and I often looked with terror at our empty food shelf.

Recently, a little hope had entered our lives. Father had obtained a small clerical job with the Liverpool Corporation. He earned only a few shillings more than the Public Assistance allowance and the extra money was swallowed up by his expenses. But it was a new beginning for him.

About the same time, we obtained a bug-ridden terrace house at a few shillings less rent than our rooms. I no longer had to face the irate complaints of the tenants in the rooms beneath us, about the noise the children made. The bugs bit unmercifully and they made a horrible smell, but the children did not complain.

I had high hopes, when Father started work, that I would be allowed to go to school and then to work, and that Mother would become the housekeeper. But Mother had obtained part-time employment as a demonstrator in various department stores, and she announced that she would be continuing this work.

'Why can't you stay at home, like other mothers do?' I implored.

'The doctor said I should work – remember?'

'Yes. But that was when you were convalescent. He wanted you to walk about in the fresh air to get strong again. But you are quite well now.'

'Oh, don't be stupid, Helen. Stop arguing. We need the money.'

'But must I always stay at home, Mummy? I'm over fourteen now. I should be at work – like other girls are. Couldn't we find someone to help out at home?'

'Really, Helen. Be sensible. How could we afford to *pay* anyone?'

We did need the money, it was true, and we never paid anybody we could avoid paying but I had all the adolescent's doubts about my elders, and I distrusted Mother's motives. There had never been much love between us. I had always been taken care of by servants; in fact, Mother had never had to take complete care of any of her children. I sensed angrily that she found it easier to go out to work than to stay at home and face the care of seven, noisy children. I found coping with six brothers and sisters, who daily became less disciplined, very hard indeed.

So, as I walked through the rain along Castle Street and absent-mindedly played with Baby Edward, and diverted Avril's attention to Minerva and then to a warehouse cat stalking solemnly across the street, I was bitterly unhappy.

We had to stop, while a desk was carried across the pavement from a furniture van into an office building; and I looked again up at Minerva.

She seemed almost to float in the misty rain, and I wondered suddenly if something more than a statue was really there, some hidden power of ancient gods that we do not understand, and I said impulsively, 'Hey, Minerva. Help *me* – please.'

The big man in a sacking apron, who was supervising the transfer of the desk, turned round and asked, not unkindly, 'Wot yer say, luv?'

I blushed with embarrassment. I must be going mad with all the strain. I'm crazy.

'Nothing,' I said hastily. 'I was just amusing the baby.'

'Oh, aye,' he replied, smiling down at Edward, while the desk disappeared through a fine oak doorway. 'You can get by now, luv.'

Chapter two

I was not quite twelve when we came first came to Liverpool, and my parents were able to keep me at home because the Liverpool Education Committee did not know of my existence. I had come from another town and did not appear in any of their records. Six weeks before my fourteenth birthday my presence in Liverpool was reported by my sister, Fiona's, school teacher. And much to my parents' annoyance, I had to attend school for those six weeks.

Now I was over fourteen, my parents had no further legal obligations in respect of my education. So, at home I stayed, simmering with all the fury of a caged cat.

I had had an aunt, a spinster, kept at home all her life to be company to my grandmother, who lived on the other side of the River Mersey. This aunt seemed to have no real life of her own, and I dreaded being like her, at the beck and call of my relations, a useful unpaid servant, without the rights of a servant. She was such a shadow of a person that I never ever thought that she might help me.

I raged to myself that I was always the last to be provided with food and clothing. I did not even think about the lack of pocket money or other small pleasures – they were beyond my ken.

In our hard-pressed family, shoes and clothing

were given first to those who had to look neat for work, and then to those who went to school. I could always manage because I did not have to go out, I was told sharply.

As housekeeper, I had to apportion the food. I fed Baby Edward first, then Avril, who was nearly five, then the two little boys, Brian and Tony. After them, frail, lovely Fiona and cheery Alan. I would then serve Father, who never complained about the small amount on his plate. What was left was shared between Mother and me. Sometimes there were no vegetables left for us, and frequently no meat, so we had a slice of bread each, with margarine, washed down with tea lacking both sugar and milk.

Mother still looked so dreadfully haggard that I would sometimes say, with a lump in my throat, that I was not hungry and would press the last remaining bits of meat and vegetable upon her. All my life I had been afraid of her tremendous temper, but such fear had long been overridden by a greater fear that she might die.

In response to my frequent complaints at not being allowed to go to work, Mother often said absently, 'Later on, you will marry. Staying at home is good practice for it.'

But I had always been assured by Mother and the servants that Fiona had the necessary beauty to be married; and I – well, I did have brains.

'You can't help your looks,' our nanny, Edith, used to say, as she scrubbed my face. 'Maybe your yellow complexion is from being ill so much. It might improve as you get older.' She used to seize a brush and scrape back my straight, mousy hair into a confining ribbon bow on the top of my head; but she spent ages curling Fiona's soft waves into ringlets.

'Why do you have to be so disobedient? You're nothing but a little vixen, you are. Nobody's going to marry a faggot like you when you grow up,' she would shout exasperatedly. 'Get those muddy shoes off, before I clout you.'

In a desperate effort to save myself from spinsterhood, I learned to obey a raised voice like a circus dog. But it did not do me much good. I was still sallow and plain, sickly and irritable.

After Father found a job, I fought a great battle with my parents for permission to attend night school three evenings a week. It became the single joy of my life. There was order and purpose in the musty, badly-lit classrooms with their double wooden desks in which, for most classes, sat more than forty pupils. The bare board floors, the faded green paint and chipped varnish were much more pleasant and clean than my home.

For the first two winters of my attendance, nobody would sit by me, because I was so blatantly dirty and I stank. Only the teachers spoke to me. In some subjects I was so behind that I needed dedicated helpers. And the teachers gave me that help.

The bookkeeping teacher taught me the simple arithmetic which I had forgotten through long absence from school. The English teachers gave me essays to write, in addition to the business letters they demanded from their other pupils. They drew my attention to poems and to essays I should read. Later,

I took German and French, and again the teacher drummed additional grammar into me, and introduced me to the translated works of foreign authors. Shorthand, a possible gateway to employment, was largely a matter of practice, and I practised zealously.

I dreamed of becoming the treasured secretary of some great man of affairs, like Sir Montague Norman, the Governor of the Bank of England, to whom I had once been introduced. He had given the silent, small girl by Father's side a new shilling, and I had curled up in an agony of shyness and refused to say thank you, much to Father's embarrassment. But, of course, when I became a secretary, I would always be ready with the correct, polite remark and flawlessly typed letters ready to be signed.

During the day, as I walked little Edward in the squeaky Chariot and, particularly after my more trying charge, Avril, had joined her brothers and sister at school, I read books balanced on the pram's raincover. I discovered Trevelyan's histories and read all those that the library had. The librarian suggested histories of other countries, so I read, not only the histories of France and Germany, but those of China and Japan, of the United States and of the countries of South America.

The heroines of some of the Victorian novels I read studied philosophy in their spare time, so I plodded through the works of several German philosophers far too difficult for me.

'Don't know what they are talking about,' I told Edward crossly.

I found a book by Sigmund Freud and decided

that he did not understand females at all. And what was it that people were supposed to be repressing all the time? Men behaved like men and women behaved like women. How could they behave any other way other than by being natural?

I tied myself up in mental knots, considering Freud, and never associated his work with the strange spasms and longings in my own maturing body. To my mind, Freud did not seem to do so well at interpreting dreams as Joseph in the Bible did.

Beneath this rabid desire for an education, for knowledge, simmered a mixture of fear and rage: I felt my parents did not really care what happened to me, as long as I continued to serve them.

Chapter three

Despite our big family, I suffered great loneliness. When Father was not too tired he would sometimes talk to me about his wartime experiences in Russia or we would discuss eighteenth-century France, of which he had a considerable knowledge. Mother ordered; she did not discuss. Without pen, ink, paper or stamps, I could not write to the school friends I had left behind in my earlier life. In fact, at first my parents refused obdurately to allow me to write.

'Why not?' I demanded crossly.

'Because it costs money, and there may be some creditors who still want to trace your Father.'

They also forbade me to write to my grandmother, Father's mother, with whom I had always spent several months of each year. Grandma, Father said, had been most unreasonable and he had quarrelled with her. I suspected that she had finally grown tired of the scandals of the gay life my parents had led before the Depression, and then of helping to pay their debts.

When I went to the local shops, I saw only older, married women, or children sent on messages, and, to me, some of the girls who lived in neighbouring streets seemed hardly human. On Saturdays and Sundays they went about in twos and threes, dressed in cheap finery. They gawked and giggled and shrieked at the gangling youths hanging uneasily about the street corners. Because their labour was very cheap, these girls had work in stores and factories. Once they were sixteen years old they usually joined their unemployed brothers.

Sometimes, when I passed a group of them as I pushed Edward along in the Chariot, they stared and laughed at me behind their hands. Garbed in the tattered remnants of my school uniform, occasionally with no knickers under the short skirt, I had to walk very uprightly lest a bare bottom be revealed to them. Once or twice they shouted at the idling boys to inquire which of them had 'caught' me. It was a long time before I realised that it was generally assumed that Edward was my illegitimate child. When I did discover it, I cried with mortification, because I knew that to have a baby out of wedlock was very wicked.

I was very vague about the origins of babies. I did not think about it very much. Dimly, uncertainly, I imagined that they came from the same place as foals and lambs and calves did. But I had never actually seen a birth and how this could be was beyond my imagining. I never equated men with stallions, rams or bulls. But, to be respectable, a child had to have a visible father or a substitute, like a gravestone, to account for his absence – that I knew. Once, when I was small, Mother dismissed our parlourmaid without a moment's notice, and I knew from the maids' gossip that she was expecting a baby – and she was not married.

Occasionally, when Edith was angry she would hiss savage remarks about my parents' lack of feeling, and quote this incident as an example of it. The house-maid left us shortly afterwards, in protest, according to Edith. Edith herself stayed with us until we left the district, because she was engaged to a young farmer nearby; and I clung to her as a mother substitute. She was a plump, comfortable country girl with rosy cheeks and fluffy, long brown hair, and was down-right in her speech. I never doubted anything she said.

I had only two close contacts to assuage this sense of isolation. One was a very old interpreter, who sometimes sat in Princes Park to sun himself. We talked a lot about the Middle East and about other languages, as I sat and supervised the children's play. One day he was missing from his usual seat and never came again. I presumed he had died and had gone to join his wife and two sons. The boys had been killed in the war and he grieved for them.

The other friend was a Spanish woman named Cristina. She and her husband, Alonzo, lived in the basement of the house next door to that in which we had originally rented an attic. Her children were all grown up and had left home. She was extraordinarily kind to Edward and me, and it was she who had given us the Chariot in which I wheeled Edward and Avril around.

In my position as surrogate mother, I had neither time nor opportunity to play. As the children became rougher and, in order to survive, became more like the other boys and girls in the district, the gulf widened between us and there seemed to be no close communication. Even Alan, so close to me in age, was to me a child; I did not worry him with details of our empty pantry.

Because I did not have a shopping bag, the greengrocer used to wrap up potatoes and other vegetables in newspaper for me, and when I arrived home I used to read these papers. There were descriptions of local tennis tournaments amongst young people, and stories of balls and receptions. I would stand dreaming with the muddy paper in my hands, imagining myself scampering about a tennis court delivering serves that raised cheers from the onlookers; or I would think how lovely it would be to skim around a ballroom in a billowing net dress. And how good it would be to go to the theatre again. In me were the stirrings of womanhood, though I did not understand them, and I had an instinctive desire to be clean, to be prettily dressed, to hide as much as possible the ugliness which I had been assured was mine.

When I thought about it, I became so afraid of the friendless, empty future, that sometimes my legs would begin to give under me, and I would have to stop walking and cling to the pram handle until the sense of blind panic passed.

Chapter four

Mother worked on short contracts in the bigger city department stores. She demonstrated new products, like kitchen gadgets, or was engaged specially to sell slow-moving goods that might deteriorate if kept in stock too long. She slowly gained a good reputation, and stores would pass her from one to another, to get rid of piles of baby baths in unpopular colours, baby clothes that threatened to harbour moths, cameras and photographic supplies left over from the summer season, and the newest wringer washers and gas stoves.

She became an excellent saleswoman, and it used to amuse me to carry Edward into a shop and watch her demonstrate the use of a gadget. It fascinated me to observe how she could beguile housewives into impulsive purchases.

One day, Avril and I stood at a discreet distance behind her in a baby-wear department. I held Edward in my arms and, though he must have known he was watching his mother, he placidly sucked his thumb and did not call out. She was selling violently pink rubber baths.

She tenderly picked up a rubber doll and plunged it into imaginary water, talking all the time, first to the doll as if it were a baby and then to her audience, who, quite amused, slowly gathered round her. She dried the doll and dusted it with baby powder and put on its nappy. Young mothers and obviously expectant mothers were her targets, and they soon found themselves hooked into friendly conversation. Mother seemed to be able to make them feel that their baby was her only interest in life; and if they already had a baby bath, she would skilfully pass them to one of the shop assistants, whose battle for a sale of baby clothes was, of course, already half won.

Before Father went bankrupt, she had for years been a member of Operatic and Dramatic Societies, and she knew enough of stagecraft to use her voice and manner to the best effect. She was never paid enough for her ability.

She looked very attractive, despite her thinness, in a black dress and black shoes purchased from a second-hand shop. I used to cut her hair for her with Father's cut-throat razor and then curl it each morning with a pair of curling tongs, bought for a penny from the pawnbroker's oddments table set up outside his shop.

Of course, I never approached her while she was working; and Avril understood that she must be quiet and tiptoe away at an appropriate moment. I doubt if she noticed that we were there, because she never mentioned seeing us.

Avril's and my great enemies were the shopwalkers. Sometimes when we were cold, we would go into a big shop and skulk around the different departments until we became warm again. And then the shopwalker would pounce.

Shopwalkers always looked very imposing. They were usually elderly gentlemen dressed in stiff, white, Victorian wing collars and black suits. They perambulated stiffly up and down the aisles of the shops, hands clasped behind their backs. They glared ferociously at the young girls and boys who served behind the counters. Then, with a slight bow, they would lend a courteous ear to customer inquiries, the whispered remarks almost drowned by the loud rings of the containers, holding payments or change, shooting along wires above their heads on their way from the counter to the cash office.

I never argued with shopwalkers.

'What do you want?' they would snarl.

'I'm just looking,' I would say loftily, exactly as I had heard people round me say.

The usual reply was, 'You can look in the windows.'

Then they would stride crossly to the nearest door and fling it open, and Edward, Avril and I would slink out like lost puppies.

One October day, we went into a shop in which Mother was working, to get warm. Mother was selling photograph albums. Her voice penetrated clearly through the murmur of shoppers as she extolled the advantages of having an album for each particular type of photograph. Avril, Edward and I settled down to watch.

I had not been feeling well for two days. My back ached, as did my head. I had got very wet in a rain storm earlier in the week, and I shrugged off the low level discomfort as being due to this. As I watched, however, the pain in my back began to feel as if an iron belt had been suddenly clasped round my waist. Pains shot down the sides of my stomach.

I gasped to Avril that we had to go home quickly, and dragged her back to the pram, parked in the shop doorway. She protested in a loud whine as I plunked her into the pram with Edward. Panting with pain, I began the long ascent up Renshaw Street, Hardman Street and Leece Street.

The pain came in ever increasing waves. Sweat beaded my forehead and I leaned on the pram handle for support, as I almost ran for home.

In St Catherine's Street, opposite the Women's Hospital, I stopped to lean against a brick wall as a particularly agonising pain ripped down the side of my stomach. Though I stared at the hospital with glazed eyes, it did not occur to me to seek succour there. To a child, in those days, hospitals were usually where old people went to die. Fiona had once gone to hospital and her lurid tales of her experiences had been enough to frighten all of the children. So the hospital was just another impersonal red brick building to stumble past on my way home.

Avril was whining and snatching at the twig with which Edward was playing. Mercifully, they both seemed unaware that anything was wrong.

I ran the pram up to the front step of our house, and tugged at the string sticking through the letter-box. The string pulled back the lock, the door swung open and I almost threw first Edward and then Avril into the narrow hall.

The pain was again surging in my stomach.

Frightened to death, I slammed the front door,

snatched up Edward and carried him through to our back yard, leaving an angry Avril howling in the hall. Perhaps if I went to the lavatory I would feel better.

I left the lavatory door ajar, so that I could watch Edward, while I snatched down my knickers.

The torn, grey garment was covered with blood.

I thought I would faint with sheer terror.

Was it appendicitis?

Again the waves of pain. I dropped down on to the seat, clasping my stomach. When the pain eased slightly, I hitched up the soaked knickers and took Edward back into the house. I had to lie down.

Avril was sitting on an upturned paint can, nursing a stray cat which had wandered in a day or two before. She had been crying and when she saw me, she let out a fresh bellow. Normally, I would have comforted her, but this time I dumped Edward unceremoniously down beside her.

'Watch Edward,' I ordered.

Where should I lie?

My bed upstairs was a door set on four bricks and I could lie on it. But Edward might follow me up the stairs and then fall down again.

Better to go into the nicely furnished front room, a place I normally did not enter because Edward was usually with me – and he always had grubby hands and was not yet reliably watertight.

Edward did follow me in, and I hastily gave him the new, unused bronze fire irons to play with. A resentful Avril stayed with the cat.

My parents, with their usual blithe inconsequence, had furnished the front room very well on the hire purchase system, regardless of the fact that the children still slept three to a bed under a motley collection of old coats and bits of blanket; and I did not even have a bed.

I was thankful enough that day, however, to curl up on the green leatherette settee. In the foetal position the pain lessened, though during the next surge I fainted.

I sobbed to myself and prayed that Mother would come home soon. Then the scarifying spasms retreated slightly and I fell into a doze.

Father shook me gently to awaken me and asked anxiously, 'Are you all right, dear? You look very white.'

My stomach and back were tight knots of pain, increasing and decreasing like waves on a seashore. I was also shivering with cold from the unheated room. I hardly dared to move, as I whimpered out the story of the torment I was enduring.

'My underneaths are bleeding, Daddy. Do you think I've got appendicitis?'

Bent over me, he listened. Then his eyes began to twinkle, his lips to twitch. A loud guffaw burst from him.

I was horrified at such a reaction to my story.

'Daddy!' I reproached him, and then broke into a moan as the pain increased.

Father straightened up and, still smiling, let out a slow sigh of relief.

'Didn't your mother explain this to you?'

'What?'

'This – this bleeding?'

'No. Was she expecting it?' I was totally bewildered, and I sobbed as the pain hit new heights.

'Well, of course. She must have been. You're a girl.'

'Of course, I'm a girl,' I gasped. 'What difference does that make? Daddy, could you get the doctor? The pain's getting worse.' I was deeply upset at his laconic attitude.

He hesitated for a moment. Then he said, 'You just stay where you are for the moment, until Mother comes home. Fiona's making the tea. I'll ask her to bring you a cup. She peeked in here and thought you were sleeping, so she has laid the table for you and cut the bread and butter. I will make the fire in the kitchen for the children.' His voice was kind.

With eyes screwed tight to help me bear the raging pain, I put my head down again on the inhospitable green leatherette. I heard him open the door, pause a moment and then say, 'Don't be afraid, old lady. This is nothing to be frightened about. You don't need a doctor.'

I did not answer him, because I did not believe him. I could not understand how anyone could be in such pain and not need a doctor. 'Mummy, come soon,' I sobbed. Cold, indifferent Mother seemed to be the key to it all.

The door clicked again and I opened my eyes. Fiona entered, carefully balancing a coarse china cup on a saucer which did not match. Despite her care, the tea slopped as she put the cup and saucer into my hand. She looked at me anxiously from beneath a roughly cut fringe of nut brown hair.

'Daddy said to drink the tea while it is very hot. What's the matter, Helen? You look awful.'

I was shaking so much that, as I raised myself a little, I slopped the tea on to the new settee. 'I don't know, Fi,' I answered, as I tried to sip the scalding liquid. 'Daddy says it's nothing – but, oh, Fi, I've got such a terrible pain in my back and tummy – and I'm bleeding underneath.'

Fiona's pink cheeks blenched. 'Bleeding?'

I nodded affirmatively. The tea was comforting and I drank it eagerly, though it was hot enough to burn my tongue.

'Oh, Helen!' she whispered.

'Daddy said to stay here till Mummy came. Can you manage?'

'Yes, of course. Daddy's making the fire and Alan is fetching the coal for him. You rest. Mummy will come soon.' She was trying hard not to panic herself.

'Where's Edward?' I asked.

'He's in the kitchen. He's fine.'

I could feel a warm trickle between my thighs and I took deep breaths to avoid screaming in fright.

'Go and have your own tea,' I told her in a strained whisper, and she went, stopping at the door to look back at me with fearful violet-blue eyes.

'Don't be afraid, Fi,' I panted and tried to muster a smile for her sake. 'I'll be all right.'

She smiled back with sudden relief and shut the door quietly after her.

I was sure, as I sank back on to the settee, that I was on my death bed. And Father did not care!

Chapter five

Mother sat down on the green leatherette easy chair opposite to me, and took off her hat. She looked tired and irritable.

'Oh, Mummy,' I wailed. 'I've got such a terrible pain – and I'm bleeding.'

'Oh, stop crying, Helen,' Mother snapped wearily. 'There's nothing the matter with you. This is what I told you about years ago. All girls bleed every month.'

I looked at her with wide-eyed horror, while I pressed my hands into my raging stomach. 'I don't remember your telling me.'

'Of course, I did – when you were about nine.'

If she had told me, the information must have been given so obliquely that it did not then register on my childish mind.

My teeth were chattering, as I asked incredulously, 'Every month – and pain like this?'

'Of course not. It doesn't hurt at all. You have just worked yourself into a panic, and that has caused the pain. It will go away quite soon. We'll try to get some aspirins, before it is due next time.'

Mother smoothed her hair, ruffled from her hat, and got up briskly. 'I'll put a kettle on and when it is boiled, you can come into the kitchen to wash yourself. I'll get a piece of cloth and show you how to keep yourself dry.'

'Will it be like this ever again?' I asked between dry sobs.

'I doubt it, if you don't have hysterics.'

Twenty minutes later, I was seated by the kitchen fire, washed and tidied, drinking another cup of hot tea. The heat from the fire helped and gradually the pain receded, as Mother had promised.

The boys stared at me because they had been told that I had had hysterics over a perfectly normal tummy ache; and they went away, Alan to night school, Brian and Tony to play bus on the stairs.

It had been a terrifying promotion to womanhood. I felt humiliated and stupid, and blamed myself for my pain. I had been aware of changes in my body, but I was so undernourished that the changes were slight and they had come slowly enough not to scare me.

Three weeks later, I collapsed with pain in night school. The English teacher made me swallow two aspirins, told me I would be all right in an hour and sent me home. Mother said the same thing and sent me up to bed, where I groaned and moaned my way through the next eight hours or so. In the early hours of the morning I fell asleep, exhausted.

From month to month the pain persisted, and Mother became more concerned. She bought dried mint and made a tea for me to drink at the onset of the first ache. It did not help. Cristina, my Spanish friend, recommended a thick paste made with ginger spice and hot water, to be licked off a spoon. Trustingly I downed this horrible concoction, but the pain continued. Cristina laughed, and said all the pain would cease either on marriage or after having a baby.

I knew I was too bad-tempered and too plain to hope for marriage; and I was certain in my mind that, however babies came, I was not going to have one outside marriage. So I smiled dimly at her and did not reply.

All the well-meaning adults in my life assured me that menstruation was just part of growing up and that some girls had more difficulty with it than others did. Nobody suggested that I should see a doctor. Since doctors cost money, and I rarely thought of acquiring anything that required payment, it did not occur to me either.

For a week or two, I would forget the pain in the bustle of caring for the children's endless needs, and running off to night school through misty streets, where strange, shadowy women lurked; and then apprehension would begin to creep over me. I would ask Mother for some of her aspirins and store them behind the alarm clock on the kitchen mantelpiece. I learned that heat was comforting and when I saw a pile of new bricks lying on a building site, I begged two cracked ones from the bricklayer and brought them home. I heated them in the oven beside the kitchen fire, and when the onslaught began I wrapped them in newspaper and lay on the green leatherette settee, clutching them close to me. Edward began to think it was a new game and wanted a brick for himself. He thought it was a great joke to cuddle up close with the bricks between us. Since he must often have been cold, the heat was probably comforting to him, too.

One freezing winter day, I fainted in the butcher's

shop. When I came round I was in an easy chair beside a fire, in the living quarters behind his little shop. His wife was forcing brandy down my throat. She must have succeeded in getting me to swallow quite a lot, because the pain did dull slightly and I felt exhilarated and yet sleepy. Edward had been propped in a matching chair on the other side of the fireplace. White rivulets down either grubby cheek marked the passage of tears. He had, however, a cheering ring of red jam round his mouth and in one hand was holding the crumbling remains of a tart.

The tiny, stuffy room was packed with furniture, and the blaze in the hearth glanced off a gilded china shepherdess on a shining sideboard opposite to me. It danced off the glass dome covering a pair of stuffed birds and made the glasses of my hostess flash.

The butcher's wife was a tiny woman dressed in the greyish, washed-out skirt, blouse and cardigan which seemed to be the uniform of women in Liverpool. Wisps of hair had escaped from her bun and draggled round a careworn face.

'Are ye feeling better?' she asked.

'Yes, thank you,' I said. I blinked at her rather hazy face through spectacles that had slipped down my nose. 'In fact, I feel fine.'

'Aye, that's good brandy, that is. You gave me husband a real fright when you keeled over.'

'I am sorry. I get a pain each month,' I faltered shyly.

She smiled. 'Oh, that was it, was it? Oh, aye. Brandy was the best thing to give you then. Does a lot for a woman at such times.'

'It seems to,' I said blithely.

Then I remembered the children's lunch, yet to be made. 'I must go home,' I said hastily. 'My brothers and sisters will be coming from school.'

'Think you'll be all right? You only live down the road, don't you?'

'Yes.'

I got to my feet. They did not feel very certain as to where the floor was; but I managed to stagger over to Edward and to pick him up. He put his arms round my neck, and sent a shower of pastry crumbs over the threadbare carpet.

Reeling slightly, I again thanked the butcher's wife. She laughed.

'It's nothing. Aye, brandy's gone to your head, hasn't it?'

'It has,' I giggled. 'But the pain is less.' I wanted to kiss her, but decided I could not aim straight. So I said effusively, 'Thank you very, very much,' and staggered, still giggling, through the lace-draped door to the shop, which she held open for me. She smiled broadly at me, as I passed.

Though sometimes the pain would rise above the effects of the brandy, and I had to stop walking and grip the handle of the old pram until the wave passed over, I hummed most of the way home. I was merrily drunk for the first time.

I rolled round the icy living room and the kitchen as I boiled and thickened the minced meat I had bought; it was as well that it was ground, otherwise it would have been unchewable. I peeled the potatoes and boiled them to a mush, before the penny in the gas meter ran out and the gas stove refused to deliver any more heat. I spread clean newspaper on the table, and laid it. Seated on a wooden chair, I waited, at first happily, for the children to come in. But as the effects of the brandy began to seep out, the chill of the dirty, comfortless room began to invade – and the pain was once more paramount.

Edward, too, was chilled and hungry and began to whimper. I took him up on my knee and wrapped us both in the old coat I used to cover him in the pram. It smelled of urine and long use. We warmed each other a little. He sucked his thumb and dozed, while I wept silently on to his scurfy little head.

I wished I had some more brandy or anything else which would stop the grinding misery within me. As I waited, I saw suddenly the expression of pain which frequently lay on my father's face – and in a burst of warm understanding I realised why he needed to drink sometimes. The burden of bereavement from the loss of most of his friends, in a war which, though it seemed a long time ago to me, was probably still quite close to him. The terror of the long, threatening winters he had spent in tiny block houses or in peasants' huts during the Russian campaign, while the Revolution surged around the tiny force, so that one did not know who was friend and who was foe—what must it have done to a delicate refined man unused to any hardship? And then to lose his fortune, his occupation, his home? He sometimes told us stories of his experiences both during the war and after it, and he made us laugh. But if one analysed those stories, they were filled with horrors.

Poor Father. I laid my head against Baby Edward's and wept not only for my own suffering, but for my father's distress as well.

Getting drunk can leave one very low afterwards, I discovered.

Chapter six

There was a silent conspiracy between Father, Mother and me, to keep from the other children as many of our troubles as possible.

We had as many creditors in Liverpool as Father had had in wealthier days. Now, instead of the tailor, the dressmaker, the grocer and wine merchant, I faced the owner of the local tobacco and newspaper shop trying to collect for the cigarettes he had supplied, the club man demanding the weekly payment for cheques issued to my parents by finance companies, for purchase of clothing at specific shops; the agent of our aristocratic landlord threatening to throw us into the street; the heavy-jowled hire purchase man growling threats to repossess our well-chosen sitting-room furniture.

Ominous clouds of danger seemed to encompass me and sometimes, after getting rid of a desperate bullying man, I would lean against the inside of the front door and cry with pure fright.

In our other life in another world, I had often heard Mother say to the parlourmaid that she was not at home to anybody, and she thus evaded personal confrontation with creditors, whose bills and threatening letters lay in the wickerwork wastepaper basket.

Here in Liverpool I had to answer the door myself. No frilly-aproned, sniggering parlourmaid stood between me and outraged men whose own livelihood was precarious. Occasionally, when I felt defeated, I would prevail on Fiona to answer the heavy bangs on the front door. She looked much younger than her age and had an expression of angelic innocence. She would say with convincing firmness, 'Everybody is out except me.'

The creditor would leave, grumbling under his breath, to mount his bicycle parked at the pavement's edge. They never shouted at her, as they did at me.

I was never given a fixed sum from which to do the housekeeping. A shilling or two was slung on to the kitchen table with instructions to buy a list of groceries for which the money was almost invariably inadequate. Consequently, Edward and I tramped for miles to save a halfpenny on a loaf of bread, or to go to a shop which would cut a twopenny, half-pound pack of margarine into quarter pounds, so that we could buy one. Stores which did this kind of splitting up of goods could, with patience, make a lot more than those which did not. A sixpenny one-pound pot of jam, sold by the ounce at a penny an ounce, assured an excellent profit. Such shops were filled with black-shawled, unwashed women and skinny, barefoot children.

We had two lots of wages coming into the house; yet no housekeeping priorities were ever established. Mother sometimes made long lists of proposed expenditures and debt repayments, but they always ended up being tossed into the fireplace. Creditors who shouted the loudest and threatened most got paid eventually; those that did not received nothing.

Cajoling credit out of shopkeepers who respected an Oxford accent was reduced to a fine art by my parents.

I can remember one pay day Mother coming triumphantly home with a box of cream cakes, when we lacked meat, milk, shoes and soap. The children, of course, thought the cakes were wonderful, and I began dimly to understand why our rough, largely Irish, neighbours spent so outrageously on weddings and funerals, cinemas and drink, whenever they got the chance. Life seemed so hopeless that they snatched at any treat, as if they had only the present and there was no future.

There was, however, a number of families nearby with less money than we had, but whose kitchen grate always seemed to have a fire in it, though it might be of slowly collected driftwood rather than of coal. Their children, friends of Fiona, Brian and Tony, were neat and clean; they ate regularly, though I cannot remember a single fat child amongst them. Their mothers obviously mended and washed frequently and could often be seen sweeping the dust out of their front doors, across the pavement and into the gutter. I often heard the sharp snap of rugs being shaken in the back yards, and saw them kneeling on the front pavement as they scrubbed and donkey-stoned their single front step. Some of them even scrubbed the pavement itself as far as the street. The menfolk were usually craftsmen or seamen, skilled with their hands. Some of them, for a couple of shillings, rented a small allotment garden from the City. These gardens were often close to railway embankments or at the edge of the city, and good crops of fruit and vegetables were raised on them during the otherwise empty summer days.

Neither of my parents had been trained to manage money. Grandpa died when Father was six. Father was sent to an excellent public school when he was ten, a school famous for the Shakespearean plays its boys enacted. He acquired a deep understanding of French and English history, and his mathematical abilities were of university level. But nobody taught him how to keep a budget or to manage a family.

Mother was equally ill-prepared for life. She was an orphan, brought up in a convent. She learned how to embroider fine altar cloths and copes; she acquired a smattering of French and other social graces, and a great love of reading. She had a fine singing voice and she learned to sing very well, though not to professional level – that would have been vulgar. The nuns who taught her hammered in the need for virtue in women, but not the basic knowledge which would make a good housewife. Since all their charges were segregated from the opposite sex, except for the skirted priests, the girls appeared to have had a wild curiosity about men and to have forgotten their lessons on virtue. Some of the girls went home to a normal family life during their holidays. But Mother's guardian was a bachelor, so she stayed at school, to spend summer holidays taking walks with the nuns and other homeless girls, and Christmases and Easters largely in church.

Unlike most of her contemporaries, Mother had had some business experience. Her guardian was the owner of a string of libraries, and when Mother became fifteen he removed her from the convent and taught her his own business. A few years later, he married. Mother was jealous of the new wife and she ran away to North Wales, where she found a post as librarian. There, she met my father during the First World War and married him.

Now we were all suffering dreadfully as a result of their frivolous, irresponsible life after the war. Even hunger, cold, sickness and pain failed to teach them to manage any better.

Poor diet produces rotting teeth, and all of us at times had to endure severe toothache. To alleviate this, we painted the offending tooth with a pennyworth of oil of cloves. Though this did sometimes ease the pain, it did not stop the tooth from deteriorating further. Then abscesses formed. Brian and Avril often sat weeping, while I applied hot poultices to their faces until the abscesses swelled and burst. Father already had false teeth when we arrived in Liverpool. But Mother's excellent teeth began to loosen from gum disease. When one became too loose, she would wiggle it with her tongue until she could pull it out with her fingers. This must have hurt her and, of course, the gaps in her mouth did not improve her looks, which must have hurt even more. Mouths full of poor teeth were, however, very common in Liverpool, and it was not unusual, particularly in respect of women, to have lost all one's teeth by the age of twenty-five.

During the second winter of attendance at night school, I found I could not see very well. I had lost some sight and my glasses needed to be replaced.

I had also grown, so that the frames were too small for me and my already plain face was made to look even more out of proportion.

A further affliction was an annoying disease called pink eye. At different times all the family caught it. It is an acute inflammation of the eye which causes a heavy discharge, so that the eyes are sealed tight during sleep and in the daytime are flushed a sickly pink. The chemist sold me tiny packets of boracic acid which we made into a solution with hot water, and it helped when we bathed our eyes with it.

But my eyes were always sore, from too much reading through wrong glasses in a bad light. Frequently we lacked pennies to push into the gas meter for the light in the living room, so I read by candlelight or, if we had no candles, I would do my homework leaning against a lamp post, to take advantage of its dim rays. The streets were lit by gas in those days, and the lamplighter would dash on his bicycle from one cast-iron lamp post to the next to pull the chain that lit the lamp. In the early part of the night school term, it was frequently warm enough for me to do my homework in the park, sitting on a bench watching the children, or there was sometimes sufficient daylight to enable me to do it at home. But the deep winter was a time to be dreaded.

I came to my studies hopelessly tired, and always hungry. The quiet order of the school, however, helped my mind to focus; and I made such a violent effort that at the end of the first year I was awarded a very small scholarship to cover the cost of books and fees for the following year. At the end of the second year, if I passed the examinations, I was to move on to a Senior Evening Institute. There the cost of books would be greater; and I had moments of panic while I waited for the results of the examinations, wondering what I would do if I did not win a scholarship this time. And even worse, what would be my fate if I failed the examination itself? My only hope would be gone.

With the exception of Baby Edward, who was still too young, the children had been sent to a local church school as soon as they reached the proper age. They attended with reasonable regularity. If I was ill, Fiona was kept at home to help, but the boys never were. I resented this blatant discrimination. Why, I often argued, was so little attention given to Fiona's and my future? A lot of anxious talk went on about careers – never jobs – for the boys. Could not girls have careers? My parents thought such remarks were funny, and they laughed. Girls got married, they said.

At night school, the other girls were talking hopefully of getting jobs as shorthand typists or as book-keepers, and some of them were already at work in shops and offices. They did not seem to be counting on having a husband to keep them, and yet they were all much prettier than me.

I used to watch them as they filed into class, usually dressed in hand-knitted jumpers and dark skirts, rayon stockings and high-heeled court shoes. Their hair was always neatly cut and sometimes Marcel waved. They used powder and lipstick generously and some of them, I noted wistfully, had necklaces, bracelets or rings.

I knew that unless a miracle occurred, I would never manage to look as nice as they did. What chance would I have of employment, even if my parents allowed me to apply for jobs? Just to get rid of the vermin on me would be a heavy task for a Fairy Godmother.

Chapter seven

At best, the years between the ages of fourteen and seventeen are not very balanced ones. Children tend to query and test the prevailing social mores, even when they have been blessed with a stable, comfortable life. Like a window pane through which a stone had been thrown, our family's life had splintered in every direction, leaving a gaping hole. Almost nothing that I had been taught as a child by Edith or by Grandma seemed to have any relevance in slums where fighting and drunkenness were everyday occurrences, where women stood in dark corners with men, fumbling with each other in a manner I was sure was wrong, though I had no inkling of what they were actually doing; a place where theft was considered smart and children openly showed the goods they had shoplifted; where hunchbacks and cripples of every kind got along as best they could with very little medical care; where language was so full of obscenity that for a long time I did not understand the meaning.

Even in my parents' light-hearted group, ideas had been discussed, theories of existence expounded, the war knowledgeably refought in the light of history. The availability of music, paintings and fine architecture had been taken for granted. Dress, deportment, manners, education, politics, were all taken seriously.

The comparison was so hopeless that I sometimes

laughed. But beneath the laughter, I seethed with suppressed rage and apprehension that even if the rest of the family managed to crawl out of their present sorry state, I would be left behind.

Like water held behind a dam shaken by an earthquake, this anger burst through my natural diffidence, one wet February afternoon, when a plainly dressed lady called at our home. Her hair was hidden by a navy blue coif, such as our Nanny used to wear; and her glasses were perched on a nose reddened by the chilly weather. She wore no makeup, and her navy blue mackintosh reached down to ankles covered in grey woollen stockings. Her black shoes, flat and frumpy, shone despite the rain. I did not recognise my fairy godmother.

When I opened the door a fraction, afraid of yet another creditor, she blinked at me in a friendly way and asked if Mother was at home.

'No,' I said cautiously, shifting Edward in my arm so that he could peep round the door, too, without my dropping him.

'And you are – ?'

'I'm Helen,' I said. 'Mother will be at home this evening, if you would like to call again then.'

The wind drove a patter of rain down the street and I heard the click of the front door of the next house as it was opened; the unemployed man next door liked to lean against his own door jamb and listen to my battles with creditors. He would stand and laugh as if he were watching a variety show, and then when it was over, would spit on to our doorstep and go indoors again.

Our visitor's eyes flickered towards the other door. Then she said, 'I wonder if I might come in for a moment. I am sure I can explain to you what I have come about.'

Reluctantly, I opened the door wider so that she could step into the muddy hallway. I heard the next door snap shut.

I ushered her into our front room. She paused on the threshold and looked round the room in obvious surprise, as she took off her gloves. The comparison between Edward's and my threadbare appearance and the pleasantly furnished room must have struck her immediately. The bugs in the walls gave it an unpleasant smell, but in the hope that they had not yet penetrated the pristine easy chairs, I invited her to sit down.

She sat down gingerly on the edge of one of the chairs, while I stood in front of her holding Edward. I did not want to put him down because his feet were bare and very cold.

She said she had come from the church to which the children's school was attached, and I nodded, though it seemed to me to be remarkable; during the two and a half years that the children had been attending the school no one from the church had called on us, and we, being so shabby, had never attempted to attend it. In fact, I had forgotten that the church existed.

Edward sucked his thumb and laid his head in the curve of my neck, so that throughout the conversation I could hear the placid slush-slush of his little tongue.

The visitor said in a bright, brittle voice that she had heard from Brian's and Tony's teachers that their singing voices were good enough for them to sing in the church choir. She had come to inquire if my parents and the boys would be agreeable to this. She knew that Mother worked part-time and she had hoped to catch her at home.

It was never possible for me to forecast what reaction my parents might have to any new situation, so I thanked her cautiously and said that Mother would be home at five o'clock.

She smiled gently up at me, but she did not get up to leave. Instead, she sighed and looked at Edward's blue bare feet.

There was an uneasy silence, and then she said in a much softer voice, 'Did you attend our school?'

'No.'

'Or the church? Have you been confirmed?'

I cleared my throat nervously and replied again, 'No.' Then, since my replies seemed abrupt, I added, 'I go to night school. I'm in Second Year Commerce.'

'Where did you go to school?'

Her face was so kind and her interest seemed genuine, so I told her about my four years in a variety of private schools up and down the country, and said rather sadly, 'I didn't learn very much. I think, if Grandma had not taught me to read and my aunt to write, I would be illiterate.'

Very slowly, while I rocked a sleepy Edward in my arms, she drew out of me the story of my struggle to go to night school, the fact that I had no clothing to speak of and the other children very little. And with a catch of self-pity in my voice, I finished up, 'There doesn't seem to be much hope for anything better for me, unless I can be free to go to work. But there is nobody to look after little Edward, if I do go.'

'But things seem to be getting better,' she comforted me. 'This room is very nicely furnished.'

'I'd rather Edward had some shoes and socks,' I retorted suddenly. 'And you should see the other rooms.'

The dam burst. 'Come and see,' I almost ordered her, and strode to the open door. 'Come and have a look.'

Without a word, her face very serious now, she got up and followed me.

Up the stairs she trudged after me, to the icy, fetid bedrooms, to inspect three iron beds with thin, old-fashioned felt mattresses on them, the urine stains uncovered by any sheet. I had tidied up the bits of blanket and old coats which we used to cover us, and some of the pillows had grubby, white pillow-cases on them.

She looked, aghast, at the door on which I slept. It was balanced on four bricks, one at each corner, and had wads of old newspaper piled on it, instead of a mattress, with a grey piece of sheeting to tuck over them. There was no other furniture, and, of course, there was no bathroom.

In a passion, I swept her downstairs again, to look at the living room, with its bare deal table, assorted straight chairs and upturned paint cans helping out as seats. The only sign of comfort was an old, wooden rocking chair and a very ancient, greasy-looking easy chair, in which was curled a stray cat which Brian had

49

earlier brought in from the rain. On the tiled floor lay a piece of coconut matting, filled with dust. In the old-fashioned iron fireplace I had laid the fire, ready for the children's return home.

The kitchen looked quite large because there was so little in it. A small table flanked the gas stove, and there was a built-in soapstone sink in one corner. The opposite corner was taken up by a brick copper, with a tiny fireplace under it, for boiling washing. Our single bucket stood under the sink; our only wash basin caught the steady drip from the house's cold water tap.

Long lines of shelves ran down one side of the kitchen. They held a motley assortment of rough, white dishes and cups, two saucepans and a dripping tin. A kettle sat on the gas stove beside a tin teapot. A small wooden table held our bits of food, a packet of tea and a blue-bagged pound of sugar, some margarine in a saucer and a new loaf.

I was shivering with cold and with emotion, and my visitor turned pitying, gentle eyes upon me. 'Don't you have a fire?' she asked. They were the first words she had spoken during our lightning tour.

'Edward and I manage during the day. I light the fire for the children coming home at lunch time, and then I re-light it for tea time.'

I realised, as I said this, that Edward and I were just as vulnerable to cold as the others were, but we remained in the frigid house while everyone else spent the day in warm buildings. No wonder my joints hurt when I moved. No wonder Edward sometimes cried because of the cold.

'Where do you keep your food?' she asked.

'On the table here,' I said. 'I buy it every day.'

She bit her lips, as she pondered over the bread and margarine, and I said a little defensively, 'Avril or Tony will fetch a pint of milk from the dairy when they come in.'

Edward had gone to sleep, so I led the way back into the living room and laid him down in the easy chair, after pushing off the cat. He stirred, but slept on, his tiny legs spread-eagled. 'I'll get something to cover him,' I told the lady, and flashed up the stairs to get a coat.

When I came back she was still standing where I had left her, and I hastily tucked Edward up before I turned again to face her. My hysterical outburst had spent itself and I felt exhausted and ashamed.

'I'm sorry,' I said, 'I should not have bothered you with all this. And I'm sorry it is not very clean – but I have nothing but a broom and cold water with which to clean – it's just impossible.'

She seemed wrapped in thought, almost as if she had not heard me. Then she smiled at me and very sweetly. 'I'm glad you did show me,' she said reassuringly. 'I can understand better the struggle you are having. Don't be discouraged – things have a way of getting better.'

I tried to smile back. I did not believe her.

'I'll come again this evening to see your mother,' she continued, a briskness in her voice.

As I let her out of the house, she turned again to me. 'Now remember. No getting discouraged.'

I nodded, then she smiled and went out into the

rain; her coif was wet before I had closed the door.

She came, as promised, and then again and again. She was a deaconess, and mother seemed to like her because she was a gentle, cultivated woman. First Brian and, later, Tony joined the choir, their white surplices saving them from the embarrassment of their shabby clothes. Later on, Tony became an altar boy, and the faith he acquired whilst kneeling in the richly decorated sanctuary never left him. He has always been an active member of the Church of England. The experience must also have helped mischievous, highly-strung Brian because, if nothing else, he learned music by many of the great composers in a bright and beautiful church. Both boys were allowed to retain the one shilling and eightpence per month paid to them for their services.

Apparently, the deaconess did not tell Mother of her tour of our house. She did, however, become an earnest advocate on my behalf. Not all fairy god-mothers carry wands.

Chapter eight

Father sometimes bought a *Liverpool Echo* to read on the tram while coming home from work. A day or two later, before using the newspaper to start the fire, I would read it, as I knelt on the coconut matting in front of the big, black, living-room fireplace.

I loved news of Royalty. Love of the royal family is still quite strong, but in those days, particularly amongst women, it was close to a passion. All our princes were officially handsome, and the courtship of Princess Marina of Greece by Prince George, Duke of Kent, was a romance about which many a girl like myself dreamed wistfully. I followed developments from day to day with eager anticipation.

I also began to read the advertisements, including the ones offering jobs. Once or twice I stole a piece of Mother's notepaper and wrote replies. I was not a very good writer but I had been taught in night school how to formulate a letter of application, which was a help. I said I had been privately educated. This was true and absolved me from having to say how few years I had been in school. It also accounted for my not having matriculated, because some girls in private schools did not attempt matriculation; they went on to finishing schools in France or Switzerland. I imagined my childhood friend, Joan, was currently attending such a school.

I told the advertisers that my appearance was neat, which was far from true, and that I was honest and hardworking and was attending evening school. With the letters wrapped in a piece of newspaper to keep them clean, I then wheeled Edward down the long hill to Victoria Street in the centre of the town and hopefully slipped the letters in the box provided by the *Liverpool Echo* for replies.

Nothing happened.

Then one day I received a reply, in handwriting far worse than my own, from a sweet shop near St Luke's Church. They wanted an assistant and asked me to come to see them the following day, a Saturday. I was dazzled at the prospect.

I hummed all day, as I waited for the evening and the return of my parents. The children found me unusually cheerful at midday, as I gave them their main meal, a half-pound of stewed, minced beef between the six of them, and mashed, boiled potatoes. They had tea to drink. Because they had a little meat, the food was an improvement over their fare during the first two years of our sojourn in Liverpool. It was also easier for me to cook it. An old gas stove was already in the house when we rented it and it worked, as long as I had the necessary penny to put in the meter. In the apartment we had first rented, I had had to cook on a bedroom fireplace, on a fire frequently kept going with scraps of rubbish culled from the streets.

Mother and Father ate their lunches in cafes or took a sandwich with them. My lunch was boiled potato. This, with the occasional addition of carrots, onions or cabbage, was my staple meal for a number of years, and it is doubtful if my parents fared much better.

Lack of nourishing food added to my parents' irritation. Mother had always had an uncontrollable temper, terrifying to maids, children and shell-shocked husband alike, and these towering tantrums reached almost insane levels during the years in which we suffered so much poverty. So I approached my parents on the subject of the letter with the care of a cat stalking a mouse.

To no purpose.

Father, at times, seemed to live in a never-never land of illusion. He looked at me over his gold-rimmed spectacles, while he sipped a last cup of tea, and said firmly that I could not be spared to go to work at present. Who would look after Edward and the children's dinner if I were absent? Perhaps, later on, he added cheerfully, I could be sent to a teachers' training college and become a school mistress. But a shop assistant? Never! That would be absurd.

I almost laughed at him. 'Which training college would consider a girl with only four years of schooling?'

His reply was drowned out by Mother's musical contralto saying firmly, 'Your place is at home, Helen. It's the most sensible arrangement. In a few years you will marry and by then Edward will be old enough to look after himself.'

I was aghast. 'But you've always said – everybody's always said – that I am so plain. How can I get married if I'm so ugly? I'll be stuck here for ever.' I began to cry, with hot, angry sobs.

I knew I looked terrible. I had seen myself once in a shop mirror. There was no greater ragamuffin in all Liverpool than me. So when Father and Mother suddenly started to talk about my getting married, I became almost hysterical. I had read fairy tales where princes materialised from all kinds of unexpected places – but the princesses were always beautiful. No prince was going to come riding by to collect a sinful, ugly hoyden like me. I had shed many bitter tears already over this fact, so successfully hammered into me by a thoughtless mother and impatient servants. I classed myself with cripples who could hope only for attractive souls, appealing to God alone.

In a paroxysm of rage all the frustration came pouring out. I raved helplessly at them, and they raved back.

I was ungrateful, thoughtless, utterly selfish. Father and Mother worked all day to maintain the family. The least I could do was to keep house. And, anyway, no matter what happened, I could not become a shop assistant. It was beneath our station.

Beside myself with fury, I ranted that Mother was working in shops. Why could not I?

The boys, with long-suffering looks, went out to play with their friends. Avril burst into tears and howled nearly as loudly as me. At such times she would go so red that even her scalp under the fine golden hair and thick scurf would flush, and she would look as if she might at any moment drop dead from apoplexy.

Fiona snatched up her ancient doll and fled upstairs.

It was night school time, but still the argument raged. Finally, I could think of no more reasons why I should go to work and I sat on a paint can, buried my face in my hands and wept uncontrollably.

Mother angrily seized some of the dishes off the table and took them into the kitchen. Father folded up the newspaper into a neat small square, a habit he had. Suddenly the room was quiet, except for miserable sobs from Avril, sitting on the floor in a corner, sturdy small legs spread in front of her. Occasionally, she would kick the tiles with her heels, as if to emphasise her misery. My own sobs were almost silent; I had long ago learned to cry without drawing attention to myself.

Mother returned from the kitchen and Father said rather carefully to her, 'Perhaps if Helen went to this shop for the interview and saw how much work a place like that would expect from her, she might realise that she is better off at home. Small places like that usually squeeze the very life blood out of their people.' He ran one finger along the newspaper's folds to neaten it, while I looked up quickly at Mother.

I swallowed a sob. Here was a tiny opening. I was sure I could do any amount of work. I conveniently ignored the fact that my physical condition was so poor that quite small exertions could make me dizzy, and each month I had to face a day of almost unbearable pain.

Between sniffs, I begged Mother in watery, meek tones, to let me do as Father suggested.

Mother had wearied herself with her tirade. She sat down suddenly and was quiet. Then she said resignedly that she had no work for the next day, so she supposed she might as well take me to see the shop. Fiona could look after Edward, since the following day was Saturday.

I had not considered that Mother might accompany me, and I had expected to have to face the interview alone. This had worried me, because I had no idea how one should behave or what one should say in such a situation, particularly as I did not want to give any indication of the kind of life we led. I felt instinctively that I would stand a better chance of getting work if it appeared that I came from a stable working class or lower middle class home, with less well-born parents than I had. What kind of an impact on a small businessman would Mother have, a lady who spoke 'with ollies in her mouth?'

I sighed, but made no objection to her coming. I said instead, 'I'd have to make myself look respectable, somehow.'

I looked at Mother hopefully. She was still dressed in her black business frock, though she had taken off her shoes and stockings and wore father's old bedroom slippers on her feet. Her face looked haggard under her make-up and her hair, which I had waved the night before, was ruffled and untidy.

Mother returned my look. 'Yes, you would,' she replied, so sharply that it sounded like an implied threat and made me jump apprehensively.

I was as tall as Mother, though with a much slighter frame, and after surveying me for a moment, she said I could borrow the dress she was wearing. Since it would be Saturday the following day, I could also borrow Fiona's black woollen stockings and black, flat-heeled shoes; Fiona was not consulted, and was very grumpy when she discovered what had been agreed. 'You'll tread them out,' she complained, 'Your feet are too big.'

'I'll be very careful,' I promised, as I recklessly washed my hair and then the rest of me in a quart of hot water in the tin basin, and used up the last sliver of soap we possessed. There would be a row with the boys in the morning about the lack of soap, but it could be endured.

I borrowed from Mother the only pair of scissors we had. She carried them in her handbag, so that they could not be misused, but even so, they were blunt and the nails on my right hand had to be finished off by biting them. Toenails were always left to grow until they broke off, and sometimes they looked like cruel, yellow claws before they finally cracked off.

The scissors were too small to cut hair, so I combed my unkempt locks with the family comb, also normally carried in Mother's handbag, and hoped it would stay off my face until the interview was over. When I received some wages, I promised myself, I would ask Mother if I could buy some hair clips.

Even after these efforts, I must have looked very odd in a black dress too long and too looose for me and without an overcoat, though it was late February and the weather was damp and chilly.

Full of hope, though shivering with cold, I trotted along beside Mother through the misty morning, past the Rialto Cinema and Dance Hall with its tawdry posters, and the dim outline of the cathedral, to the sweetshop.

It was a very little shop, in a shabby block of other small shops and offices. Its window, however, sparkled with polishing despite the overcast day. Through the gleaming glass I could dimly see rows of large bottles of sweets and in front of them an arrangement of chocolate boxes, all of them free of dust. Beneath the window, a sign in faded gold lettering advertised **Fry's** Chocolate.

Mother, who had not spoken to me during the walk, paused in front of the shop and frowned. Then she swung open the glass-paned door and stalked in. I followed her, my heart going pit-a-pat, in unison with the click of Fiona's shoes on the highly polished, though worn, linoleum within.

An old-fashioned bell hung on a spring attached to the door was still tinkling softly when a stout, middle-aged woman with a beaming smile on her round face emerged through a lace-draped door leading to an inner room.

'Yes, luv?' she inquired cheerfully.

'I understand that you wrote to my daughter about a post in your shop?' Mother's voice was perfectly civil, but the word 'post' instead of 'job' sounded sarcastic.

The smile was swept from the woman's face. She looked us both up and down uncertainly, while I agonised over what Mother might say next.

'Helen?' the woman asked, running a stubby finger along her lower lip.

'Helen Forrester,' replied Mother icily.

'Ah did.' The voice had all the inflections of a born Liverpudlian. She looked past Mother, at me standing forlornly behind her. Her thoughtful expression cleared, and she smiled slightly at me. I smiled shyly back.

I felt her kindness like an aura round her and sensed that I would enjoy being with her, even if she did expect a lot of work from me.

'Have you ever worked before, luv?' she asked me, running fingers on which a wedding ring gleamed through hair which was improbably golden.

I nodded negatively. Then cleared my throat and said, 'Only at home.'

'What work would Helen be expected to do?' asked Mother, her clear voice cutting between the woman and me like a yacht in a fast wind. She had also the grace of a yacht in the wind; but the sweet-shop owner was obviously finding her more trying than graceful and answered uncertainly, 'Well, now, I hadn't exactly thought. I need a bit o' help, that's all. 'Course she'd have to wash the floor and polish it, like, every day. And clean the window and dust the stock. And when I knowed her a bit she could probably help me with serving, like. I get proper busy at weekends – and in summer the ice cream trade brings in a lot o' kids, and you have to have eyes in the back o' your head or they'll steal the pants off you.'

Mother sniffed at this unseemly mention of underwear, and then nodded.

'And what would the salary be?'

I groaned inwardly. I was sure that in a little shop like this one earned wages not a salary.

61

The beginning of a smile twitched at the woman's lips, but she answered Mother gravely.

'Well, I'd start her on five shillings, and if she was any good I'd raise it.'

Even in those days, five shillings was not much. The woman seemed to realise this, because she added, 'And o' course, she can eat as many sweets as she likes. But no taking any out of the shop.'

I could imagine that this was not as generous as it sounded. After a week of eating too many sweets, the desire for them would be killed and few people would want them any more.

Mother inquired stiffly, 'And how many hours a week would she work for that?'

'Well, I open up at half past seven in the morning to catch the morning trade, you understand. And I close up at nine in the evening.' She paused a moment and then said, 'But I wouldn't need her after about seven o'clock. Me husband's home by then, and he helps me after he's had his tea. And I close Wednesday afternoons, so she'd have the afternoon off after she'd tidied up, like. Me husband helps me Sundays, too, so I wouldn't want her then either.'

I wanted the job so badly that I did not care how many hours I worked, how often I scrubbed the floor. The shop seemed so lovely and warm, after our house, and I sensed that in a rough way the woman would be kind to me. I tried to will the woman to agree to take me.

A little boy burst through the shop door, leaving the bell tinging madly after him. He pushed past us and leaned against the corner of the counter.

'Ah coom for me Dad's ciggies,' he announced, turning a pinched, grubby face up towards the sweet-shop owner.

'Have you got the money?'

'Oh, aye. He wants ten Woodbines.' A small hand was unclenched to show four large copper pennies.

The cigarettes were handed over and the pennies dropped into the wooden till.

'Now don't be smoking them yourself,' admonished the woman, with a laugh.

The boy grinned at her and bounced back to the door, his bare feet thudding. As he went through the door, he turned and gestured as if he were smoking.

'Aye, you little gint!' she said.

The interruption had given Mother time to make a rapid calculation. As the woman turned back to her, she said sharply, 'There is a law about how many hours a minor can work – and, incidentally a law about selling cigarettes to minors. I am sure that over sixty hours a week – at less than a penny an hour – are far more hours than are allowed.'

The woman shrugged huffily; her eyes narrowed, giving her a cunning expression.

'I'm sure I don't know about that,' she replied tartly. 'If she doesn't want the job she doesn't have to take it. There's others as will be grateful for it.' She sniffed, and looked at me disparagingly. 'Anyway, I wouldn't take her. The sores on her face would put the customers off. I got to have a clean looking girl.'

I looked at her appalled, hurt to the quick. In front of our broken piece of mirror, I had carefully squeezed each pimple on my face, so that the acne

63

was temporarily reduced to raised red blotches with a fresh, golden scab on each. I had no make-up to cover the results. But I had hoped that I looked clean.

Mother's face flooded with angry colour. For a moment she looked like Avril in a tantrum. She cast a scornful glance at the shopkeeper, who stared back at her with her chin thrust upwards, quite unabashed.

'Good afternoon,' Mother snapped, as she swung round and opened the street door. The little bell tinkled crossly at being so forcibly disturbed.

'Helen, this way.'

It was an order, and I slouched out through the doorway, closely followed by my wrathful mother.

Chapter nine

Mother scolded sibilantly all the way home, and blamed me for wasting her time. I was too crushed and disappointed to respond.

Back I went to the kitchen and little Edward, who trotted patiently by my side, while I fumed miserably. In saner moments, I acknowledged that Mother had saved me from savage exploitation. But her motives in doing so were, to me, suspect. And as the years went by I felt that my increasing efficiency at home was daily making more certain that I stay there. Probably a few pennies of pocket money or a modicum of praise would have done much to soothe me. But everything I did was taken for granted. Failures were bitingly criticized. There was no one to turn to for consolation, except, occasionally, to Fiona.

And yet I yearned to love my parents and be loved in return, to have with them the tender relationship I had had with Grandma during the long months I had frequently spent with her during my childhood. But Grandma had vanished with the rest of my friends. In my innocence, I did not understand that my parents' fast and extravagant life in the post World War years had alienated every relation they had. Father's widowed mother – the last to desert them – had left her son to learn the hard way the teachings she had failed to inculcate in him when young. She probably had no conception of the depth of our sufferings.

There is no doubt that Mother never forgave her friends for deserting her after Father went bankrupt; it was as if she declared a silent, ruthless war against her own class. The depth of her bitterness was immeasurable.

I remembered well the doll-like creatures who used to frequent our drawing room and dining room. In short, beige georgette dresses, their Marcel-waved hair covered by deep cloche hats, they teetered on high heels in and out of our old home in considerable numbers. Afternoon tea or dinner were served by a parlour maid in black and white uniform. Sometimes well-tailored young men, who also had time to waste, came to drink a cocktail or have a cup of tea.

Several times, a man vanished from the usual circle. One of the ladies would say, between puffs on a cigarette held in a long holder, 'Gas, dahling – his lungs couldn't stand it,' or 'He was loaded with shrapnel – a piece moved round to his heart. Too utterly devastating.'

I was allowed to attend the tea parties. Edith would dress me in my best frock, usually shantung silk, long white socks and brown lace-up shoes, and I would sit and nibble a piece of cake and watch the prettily dressed visitors. I soon learned that most of the men were unemployed, ex-army officers; they usually had some private means left them by more enterprising forefathers, but as prices rose their money shrank. They had no special qualifications and sought jobs as car salesmen or vacuum cleaner salesmen. One of them regularly allowed me to reach up and touch the silver plate the doctors had implanted to replace the top of his skull; another had an artificial leg which creaked when he walked. Father himself had trouble with his hands, which had been frost-bitten during his service in Russia. He also got chest pains, forerunners of the heart attacks to come.

So, perhaps my parents' friends, bereaved, disillusioned, wounded in a war of frightful, unnecessary suffering, had so many troubles of their own that they were unable to help one of their number who had failed largely through his own inadequacies.

I was born after the war, so it was only history to me. Had I realised, when I got so cross with my parents' ineptitude, how close it still was to them, how they had already gone through the shock of seeing the kind of life they understood crumble, I would have been much more compassionate.

One windy March evening, when the children's need of clothing seemed particularly dire, Mother decided to write to some of her old acquaintances to ask for second-hand clothing. After all, she said bitterly to Father, the most she could lose was a three-halfpenny stamp, since she appeared to have lost any friendship there was.

When the children had gone to bed, she sat at one end of the living-room table and wrote three letters, while I sat at the other end and did my homework.

Three days later, a scented letter dropped through our letter box. As far as I could remember, it was the first letter, other than a bill, which we had received since coming to Liverpool.

Opening it was a ceremony, carried out under the eager eyes of the entire family.

'It's from Katie,' said Mother, naming a gay, childless married friend, as she slit the envelope with the kitchen knife.

It contained a single sheet of notepaper wrapped round a five pound note. Katie was sorry about us and sent the enclosed with love. Mother had found a technique for adding to our income.

Until she had exhausted every possible person she could think of, Mother wrote at least one begging letter a week. She rarely got money out of the same person twice. But she had had an enormous circle of acquaintances, and when she ran out of these she wrote to the parents of the children's friends and also moving letters to their teachers. After that, she wrote to people whose names she had picked out of library reference books.

She learned to write eloquently of the children's woes and her own efforts to find work. She did not mention Father in letters to strangers, perhaps to give the impression, without actually saying so, that she was widowed. She frequently passed her efforts over to me to read – one of the few times when she took me into her confidence. I had never heard of confidence tricksters and I read them admiringly, believing them to be a perfectly honourable way of earning money. After all, Grandma had always said that charity was a great virtue, and we were certainly in need.

There were many professional begging letter writers in Liverpool at that time. Earnest gentlemen sat in their tiny bed-sitting rooms and wrote passionate appeals for help to any monied person who came to their attention. They invented whole families of starving children, aged parents in need of shoes, wives dying of tuberculosis, and so on. And they made a steady living at it. In contrast, Mother could say honestly that her children were in dreadful need, even if bad management was part of the cause of it.

Some well-to-do people, including Royalty, who were bedevilled by begging letter writers, would send the letters to a charitable organisation in the city, with the request that they investigate the need; it was remarkable how generous people were when the need was found to be genuine. I do not recollect, however, anyone coming to investigate us as a result of one of Mother's letters.

Thanks to the kindness of many people unknown to me, a few comforts began to trickle into the house, amongst them a second-hand iron bed for me. The spring was hollowed out like a hammock and it was a number of years before I acquired a mattress. I shared it for a while with Edward, but it represented my first personal gain at home since we had arrived in Liverpool. It was at least another five years before I got proper blankets and sheets for it; and lying chilled to the marrow through endless winter nights was one of the greater hardships for all the children.

Sometimes parcels of clothing or bedding arrived in response to the letters. Clothing for the younger children was almost invariably given to them and it helped to keep them tidy for school. Sometimes there was clothing which fitted Mother; men's clothing was rarely sent, perhaps because of the difficulty of fitting.

The bedding was usually bundled up with some of the clothing, ready for pawning.

Seared by disappointment, I would take the cloth-wrapped parcel to the crowded pawnbroker's shop with its three golden balls hanging in front of it, and, after much good-natured haggling with the pawnbroker, I would receive four or five shillings, and a ticket so that I could later redeem the parcel.

The parcel was whisked away from the high, black counter and thrown up a chute to the pawnbroker's assistant in the store room above. After a year, if the goods had not been redeemed or interest paid on the loan, the parcel would be torn open and the contents sold. So many goods were for sale that the pawnbroker's was an excellent place to buy almost anything, from clothing and boots to an engagement ring or a bedspread or a concertina; and there were always women wrapped in shawls or in long, draggling men's overcoats, picking through the merchandise on the bargain tables set out in front of the store on fine days.

The money raised from the pawnbroker might be used for a little extra food or, more frequently, to pacify a creditor who had threatened court procedure. Cigarettes were almost always one of the first things bought with it, and sometimes Mother would go to the cinema. She often remarked angrily that if Father could afford a drink, she could afford a cinema seat.

The local newspaper-shop proprietor, after a fierce row with me because Father owed him a whole pound for cigarettes, obtained a Court Order against us. This meant that the bill had to be paid by regular instalments set by the Court, on threat of the bailiffs selling us up if we failed to pay. This added enormously to my fears, because I had stood and watched while whole houses of furniture were sold by the bailiffs for a few shillings to settle a ridiculously small debt. Mother once bought for sixpence a superb hand-made rocking chair when there were no other bids for it.

I never knew where my parents might run up another bill or who might pounce on me, as the hapless housekeeper who had to answer the door. I had always been afraid of people who shouted, and I would stand shivering with my shoulder against the inside of the door, while someone hammered and shouted on the outside.

Once or twice I considered running away, but in those days there was no support from welfare organisations for such a runaway. And who would employ someone like me?

I once threatened to go to Grandma, but my Father said grimly that she would probably turn me away, that I should be thankful for what I had. Things would get better one of these days.

Grandma had become a loving, distant dream to me, and I was shocked beyond measure at the idea that she no longer cared. Yet I believed what Father said.

Chapter ten

Spring had come at last. The trees lining Princes Avenue were stickily in bud; the privet hedges behind the low, confining front walls of the houses were already bursting into leaf, and the sparrows and pigeons were a-bustle with the need to mate.

I wheeled Edward down Parliament Street to the small Carnegie library in Windsor Street. A playful wind flipped dust and pieces of paper round its railings, against which women leaned, shopping bags on arm, to gossip in the pale sunshine. The soot-covered library was a handsome little building with high, arched windows which made it pleasantly light inside. Its battered books passed through my hands at the rate of about half a dozen a week and helped me to forget hunger, cold and humiliation. The librarians knew me and sometimes recommended a new book which had come in. In those days, librarians seemed to be great readers and both Father and I enjoyed discussions with them about books we had read.

I parked the Chariot close to the iron railings at the front. Edward was a patient child who would sit and watch the passers-by while I hastened to find something new to read.

As usual, I went directly to the section devoted to travel books. A new travel book was a great treat to me, I learned all I know of geography from them. I would carefully follow on the maps in the books journeys through countries as diverse as Tibet and Bermuda, examining myopically photographs which ranged from very fuzzy to very clear. I was always annoyed when there was no map in the book because I did not have an atlas, and poor photography was also a great disappointment. Later, more affluent generations would travel by hitchhiking the routes my fingers traced so longingly on maps.

I pushed my straggling hair back behind my ears and took off my faulty glasses to peer closer at the shelves; sometimes I could see better without the glasses than I could with them.

'Helen Forrester, isn't it?' inquired a voice from behind me.

I turned slowly, surprised that anyone should know me by name.

It was the deaconess from the church, to whom in a rage I had shown our house. It was no wonder that I had not recognised her voice. During our previous encounter, she had said so little while I had said so much. I blushed at the memory of my unpardonable outburst.

I murmured shyly that I was Helen. She looked very sweet in her coif and frumpy clothes.

'I was about to come to see you,' she announced unexpectedly. Then she glanced round the book-lined room. 'Perhaps we could talk here, though. Let's go over there.' She took my elbow and guided me into a corner of the Fiction section.

'I wanted to ask you, my dear, if you would like a

job as a telephonist. A charity I know of needs a girl, and I immediately thought of you, because you have such a pleasant voice.'

I gaped at her, struck dumb by the unexpectedness of the offer. Then I gasped, 'Oh, yes.'

She smiled at me, and continued, 'The salary is not much – about twelve and sixpence a week. Would you like me to arrange an interview for you?'

Twelve shillings and sixpence a week seemed a huge sum to me. All the wonderful things it would buy danced before me, mixed with a terrible apprehension that I would not get the job because I was so dirty and had no clothes except the grubby, ragged collection I was wearing.

The deaconess was talking. 'I thought I would ask you first, before speaking to your mother.'

At the mention of Mother, I remembered the sweet shop episode.

'My parents will never agree to it,' I said hopelessly. 'I have to look after Edward.'

'I've already thought of that,' she responded eagerly. 'Alice Davis lives a few doors away from you. She has an invalid mother who cannot be left alone and she badly needs to earn a few shillings. I am sure she would take care of Edward during the day – and she wouldn't charge much.'

A fairy godmother in a blue coif! A true fairy godmother. A wave of gratitude surged through me, but I did not know how to express it. 'Would she, really – would she do it?' I whispered.

'I'm sure she would, if I ask her.'

I was acquainted with Alice. She belonged to the

Salvation Army. I said 'good morning' to her most Sundays, as she strode along the street pushing her mother's wheelchair down to the Citadel. Her mother would be bundled up in rough grey blankets, regardless of whether it was winter or summer; and Alice wore a navyblue uniform, with a matching Victorian bonnet trimmed with a red ribbon proclaiming 'Salvation Army' across the front. Her sturdy legs were clad in sensible black stockings and the shine on her black shoes equalled that on the shoes of our local police constable. Her cheerful face shone like her shoes. Occasionally, the Salvation Army band played at the end of our street, and Alice would rush down to them, clutching her cymbals, ready to join in while they were so close to her home. Alice was rough, but Edward would be safe with her.

Please, Lord, please let it happen, I prayed silently. Aloud, I said, 'Thank you very, very much. I would love the job if you think I can do it.'

She smiled. 'Of course you can do it. Shall I call on Mrs Forrester tonight? You might like to talk to both your father and your mother first.'

'I will,' I said, though I had no real hope. Perhaps, however, with an advocate like this respectable lady, just perhaps, they could be persuaded.

'I'll come this evening, then?'

'Yes, please,' I mumbled.

In a daze, I wheeled Edward home, pushing the pram unseeingly through the usual crowds of black, white and yellow men idling at the corners. Some of them murmured resentfully as the pram brushed carelessly past them.

How on earth was I to approach Mother and Father about this offer? I worried. A chance of freedom at last, a tiny flame of hope in a very bleak world.

The whole routine of the family would have to be altered. Alan and Fiona would have to shoulder some of my work. And Alice would have to be paid. Some clothes would have to be redeemed from the pawnbroker – or obtained from somewhere else. Where would Mother find the money?

At home, I poked up the fire and began to make toast for the children's tea, while I thought once again of running away. Could I live on twelve shillings and sixpence? Boys sometimes ran away to the south, where there was more work than in financially ruined Liverpool. Occasionally, girls did, too. I had, however, read in the newspaper about the flourishing white slave traffic into which girls were sold. I was not clear what happened to white slaves, except that they were kept in bondage and abused by ruthless men until they died. I imagined them being misused like American black slaves, and I had no wish to die a dramatic death like Uncle Tom in *Uncle Tom's Cabin*. I had wept over this tragedy as a small girl and did not wish for a similar fate.

I did some careful arithmetic. A small, unheated housekeeping room could be found for about seven shillings and sixpence a week; food, say, four shillings, firing in winter would take the other shilling, leaving nothing for clothing. I did not consider that I might need tram fares – I had been walking, now, for the past three years all over south

Liverpool; make-up was beyond my experience, and pocket money an idle dream, anyway.

The children drifted in for tea and I dealt with their squabbles and their hunger as best I could.

Father and Mother returned from work soon after the children. Inside five minutes, they were quarrelling violently. I cannot remember what triggered the trouble. It did not matter, because the underlying animosity smouldered all the time and needed very little to make it flare up. As usual, they drew each child into the argument in an effort to make them take sides, and this frequently reduced Avril and Brian to hysterics as they agonised between the parents. Fiona and Alan were old enough to retreat to friends' homes if they got desperate enough, but poor Avril, Tony and Brian had no such refuges. Tony usually managed to stay a little calmer, though he was always upset, and Edward just stuck firmly in whichever lap he happened to be cradled when hostilities broke out.

Even when I was very small, I wondered why my parents stayed together. I knew a girl whose mother was divorced, and I quite envied her. But I had been fortunate in having Edith to take care of me and there were the long absences from home when I stayed with Grandma. In their conversations about the people they knew, they taught me that not all families were riven by warfare. Now, as the fight raged over the tea table, I wished passionately I could run to Grandma for help.

Alan had piled into the fight with some furious, rude remark and was sharply slapped by his father.

He shot out of the kitchen door into the back yard, raging nearly as incoherently as Father was.

Fiona wept helplessly, her head on the table. Brian and Tony stonily munched their toast, their movements nervous and uncoordinated; they did not answer the passionate appeals of Mother and Father to take their side. Avril stood behind Mother's chair, holding on to it and shaking it, as she shouted hopelessly, 'Stop, everybody. Why can't you stop?'

Neither protagonist would give way.

I was silent with despair. I hardly heard the words hurled around me or addressed to me. What was I going to do when the church lady arrived? Mother seized a cup and saucer from the table and hurled them into a corner. Through her screams of rage, I heard a knock on the front door.

The other children had also heard the sharp rat-tat. When they instinctively turned their heads towards the front of the house, Mother stopped in mid-scream.

'What was that?' asked Father, his lips turned back in a snarl.

'Someone is at the door,' I said, too much in anguish to move.

'Well, get a move on, girl. Answer it. Say we are not at home.'

Reluctantly I obeyed, feet dragging. I shut the living-room door behind me.

As I turned the lock on the front door, I wished, for the first time, that it was only a creditor. The moment I swung back the door, she was in the muddy hall and pulling off her gloves, as the wind gusted behind her.

'It's quite cold this evening,' the deaconess said cheerfully. 'Well, have you asked them, my dear?'

'I haven't had an opportunity yet,' I apologised.

Her smile faded, and she sighed. 'Never mind. I'll ask for you.'

'They said they are not at home tonight.'

From behind the closed door came the sound of renewed strife, though the level seemed more subdued. The interruption had broken the continuity of the argument. The lady laughed and looked at me conspiratorially. The living room was suddenly quiet. The feminine chuckle must have penetrated to the family.

The deaconess tucked her gloves into her handbag and said briskly, 'I imagine your mother would be at home to me. We know each other well enough to call occasionally without warning, don't we?'

I tried to smile at her as I heard the living-room door open behind me. 'Will you come into the front room?' I asked hastily. 'I'll inquire if they are at home.' These were phrases I had often heard May, our parlourmaid, use, and they came automatically to mind in such a difficult situation.

I opened the door to the front room and ushered the blue-clad lady into it, just as Avril stumped out of the other room, her eyes tearful, her mouth surrounded by black toast crumbs. She marched into the sitting room after the visitor, and stood staring at her.

I heard the deaconess speaking softly to the frightened little girl, as nervously I announced our visitor to Mother and Father. Both parents were standing motionless, like alerted hares, as they tried to judge who the visitor was.

Mother, her face and neck still red from combat, pushed past me and went into the front room. Father gave a great sigh and flopped into a chair. His hands were trembling as they always did when he was upset.

Fiona had ceased to weep and gazed up at me with great pansy eyes still dewdropped. Brian and Tony asked Father's permission to leave the table.

'Yes,' he said peevishly.

They scrambled down from their chairs and I heard the back door slam, as they went out to play in the last of the evening light.

Father turned back to me. He gestured with his head towards the front room. 'What does she want?' he asked. I think he was always nervous that his wife had done something outrageous which he did not know about.

I knelt down on one knee and began to pick up the bits of cup and saucer that Mother had shattered. Through my draggling hair, I hesitantly answered him.

'She has come about me.'

He sat up straight and looked at me. 'About you? What have you done?'

I stood up and faced him. 'I haven't done anything. She's got a job for me. And she's keen that I should take it.'

'What nonsense!' He sniffed, and then added angrily, 'I wish she would mind her own business.'

'She means well, Daddy.'

'She should hie her back to her nunnery and stay there. She has no right to interfere with my family.' He thumped the arm of his chair. 'She has no right to put ideas into your head.'

I stood irresolutely before him, the broken dishes in my hand. I wanted to put my arms round him and beg him to intercede for me. When I was small and he was not too busy, we had been able to talk to each other. But this ease between us had got lost in the maelstrom of trouble which had engulfed us. So I hesitated, and the opportunity was lost.

'Where is the newspaper?' he demanded irritably.

I put down the broken china and picked up the paper from the floor, where it had been thrown down during the quarrel. He shook out the pages and vanished behind them.

Chapter eleven

Washing greasy dishes in cold water without soap is not easy. The grease impregnates the hands and forms an oily ring round the basin. I had two saucepans left over from lunchtime to wash, and their exteriors were covered with soot from the fire. To save the gas, I had put the pans on the living-room fire to finish the cooking of the children's midday dinner. Now the soot floated revoltingly amid the grease. I did not dare to put a kettle of water on the fire as I was afraid of irritating Father further by pushing past him. I let the water from the single cold water tap cascade into our tin wash basin to sweep out some of the soot, and stood gazing at the backs of my hands in the light of the candle I had just lit.

My hands were small and well-formed. The skin was ingrained with dirt and round the quicks the nails were almost black. The nail tips were long and uneven and filled with grime. Sometimes I tried to clean my nails with a sliver of wood, but without plenty of soap it was a hopeless task. I remembered the scathing remark of the sweet-shop lady, and, with a stomach clenched with apprehension, I realised that to make myself thoroughly clean and neat for work would be very difficult.

In a painfully sweet voice, Mother suddenly called me from the front room, and I was jolted back from depressing contemplation to frightening reality.

I wiped my hands on the family's solitary towel which hung on a hook on the back door. The towel was nearly black from use by nine people and it invariably stank. I added a streak of soot to it.

Father had joined Mother and the deaconess, Miss Ferguson, in the front room, and was perched uncomfortably on the edge of one of the easy chairs. I could feel the blood draining from my face; and, as I gave Miss Ferguson a nervous smile, I wanted to faint.

'Miss Ferguson insists on hearing from you personally that you do not want to go to work,' announced Mother frigidly, and Miss Ferguson shifted uncomfortably around in her chair. 'I understand she spoke to you in the library this afternoon.'

'Yes, she did,' I whispered, in answer to the second statement.

Miss Ferguson took a large breath, as if the effort to speak was going to be too much for her. Then she turned her worried-looking face towards me, and said very carefully, 'I have been trying to persuade Mr and Mrs Forrester that it would be greatly to your advantage if you could go to work and be trained for some worthy occupation, and that it would be possible for them to spare you from the house to do this. I tentatively made an appointment for you for tomorrow afternoon at three o'clock.'

Father made a wry face, and I had the feeling he wished he was a hundred miles away.

Mother interjected, 'Helen will not be keeping the appointment, I am sure.'

Undeterred, Miss Ferguson pressed on. 'I have assured your mother that you will be working with nice women, all from good families, and I am sure you will be well trained.' She turned to Father and said very earnestly, 'She would be quite safe there,' as if any other place of work was probably a cesspool of immorality.

Father was embarrassed. 'I don't doubt it,' he muttered, and looked across at Mother.

I looked down at my hands resting on the back of the easy chair, and burst into tears. It was easy to see that my parents were boiling with suppressed anger at the intrepid little deaconess's foray into our affairs. They would raise hell when she was gone. I put my head down on my hands and cried until the tears ran through the fingers on to the shiny green leatherette of the chair.

Avril, who had been sitting on a matching poof, sucking her thumb and watching the proceedings very quietly, suddenly started to cry as well, and was immediately whisked into the hall and the door shut on her. I could hear her wailing in the dark.

'Don't cry, Helen,' said Father ineffectually.

Mother turned to Miss Ferguson, as she shut the door after Avril.

'Helen is obviously very upset, Miss Ferguson. Perhaps we should discuss the matter with her and let you know in a day or two what has been decided.'

I was not just upset; I was nearly out of my mind with despair. But the tears came with such tremendous force that I could do nothing to stop Miss

Ferguson being quickly, though politely, eased out of the house.

When I heard the latch on the front door click shut, I flung myself wildly on to the settee and continued to sob. What was the use of a day or two, when the appointment was for tomorrow?

It was fortunate that Father and Mother had already exhausted themselves with one quarrel that evening, and Mother, therefore, contented herself with ordering me to control myself, while Father asked how they could talk to me when I was making such a racket.

I made a violent effort, sat up and dried my face with the backs of my hands.

Mother looked so terribly exhausted, when finally I lifted my eyes to look at her, that I felt an overwhelming guilt and said, 'I'm sorry, I really am.'

Mother had been dreadfully ill just before we arrived in Liverpool. She had had no real care since then, so that she was soon drained of strength. I truly did not want to add to her hardships; yet I could not bear my present miseries much longer.

'Have you been talking to Miss Ferguson or to the Fathers at the church, behind our backs, Helen?' asked Mother. There was an implied threat in the question. Family affairs, we had been taught from infancy, were not discussed with servants or outsiders. Childish revelations, whenever discovered, had been dealt with by a sharp spanking or, sometimes, caning.

I was too upset to care or remember about Miss Ferguson's tour of our house, so I said indignantly that I had not. I took off my glasses and wiped them down the front of my gym slip, while I tried to think how my going to work could be managed.

'You know, Daddy,' I said, approaching the weaker partner, 'the salary offered is quite good. It would mean three salaries coming into the house.'

'Alice Davis wants ten shillings a week to look after Edward,' interrupted Mother. 'And there are still the other children's needs.'

'Surely if everybody helped, we could manage between us. It wouldn't hurt Fiona and Alan to help – they are quite big now.'

Mother dismissed Fiona and Alan with a gesture.

'On Sundays I could clean the house, and, if Fiona and Alan could make the tea, I could put Edward and Avril to bed when I came in.'

'It is not very practical,' Father said. 'Someone has to be at home to make the children's lunch.'

My temper was rising, that incorrigible devil which dwelt within me. I fought it by praying each night that I would manage to keep calm until prayers the following night, and so often I failed. I made tremendous efforts to control it, not realising that insufferable people and unbearable circumstances could make a saint angry.

I stood up and flounced towards the door.

'I am going for the interview, whether you like it or not. I may never get such a chance again. I must take it.'

'Helen, you forget yourself,' exploded Father.

'Oh, no I do not. For once, I am remembering myself.'

'Helen!'

Mother's voice came in behind him. There was more than a little malice in her tone, as she said, 'You have no suitable clothing, anyway.'

'I'll borrow some,' I replied recklessly.

'Helen! That would not do at all.' Father sounded genuinely shocked.

'It's no worse than borrowing money,' I retorted, and his face whitened. I had hit home most cruelly. Savagely satisfied, I fled from the room and back to the sooty saucepans.

Chapter twelve

I peeped over the railings surrounding the area. The curtains had not yet been drawn over the barred windows of my dear Spanish lady's basement living room. In the soft light of her oil lamp, I could see her sitting in an easy chair on one side of the fireplace, with a pile of crochet work on her lap. Her handsome, black-eyed husband, Alonzo Gomez, sat opposite her on another easy chair. He was reading the newspaper, while a large black cat crouched on his shoulder, its lemon-shaped eyes glowing in the light. The remains of their evening meal still lay on a nearby table.

I opened the iron gate and ran down the winding iron steps of the area, knocked at the plank door under the main entrance steps of the house and, after waiting a moment, walked in.

I was engulfed by skinny brown arms and a flood of mixed Spanish and English words of welcome. Alonzo put down his paper as I entered their living room.

'Come, come,' he said, gesturing towards the blazing fire with one hand, while he smoothed his handlebar moustache with the other. He got up and bowed me to his chair.

Suddenly, I was in a different world.

Despite the general squalor, there were many

people like Cristina Gomez who created real homes out of attic crannies or damp basements in once fashionable houses. There was never much money, though Alonzo Gomez worked as a carter for a fruit merchant in the city and the couple's children were now grown up and had moved away; and yet the old kitchen had an air of cosiness, as if affection was exuded from the walls with the damp. The few pieces of well-worn furniture, the primitive cooking utensils hanging by the fireplace, the stone floor covered in the centre by a piece of coconut matting, all were clean and well cared for. Alonzo was known to have an explosive temper, but the explosions seemed to be rare, and at other times there was a lot of good-natured banter and teasing, when they laughed like children.

Cristina Gomez had a good collection of clothing. She had once told me that whenever her husband earned overtime money or won on the horses, he would spend the money on clothes for one or the other of them. And now I needed to borrow a whole outfit.

All Cristina's clothes were black, even her petticoats, but that would not matter. Black was the uniform of work. It was usually worn by shop assistants and by many office workers.

After I had been cuddled and installed in Alonzo's chair, while he sat on a straight-backed one, an orange was sliced and put on a saucer and a cup of strong, black coffee set before me on a brown-painted orange box. The health of all the family was inquired after by Cristina, and Mother's poor health sighed over with much rolling of eyes and shrugging of shoulders.

At the mention of Mother's health, my determination faltered. If I went to work, her load would inevitably be increased. Then, as Alonzo told a funny story about a cart horse which loved to steal apples from displays outside the Fruit Exchange, I realised that, on average, Mother did not earn much more than I would get, that if she stayed at home to look after the family, we would be very little poorer. And my resolve hardened.

Cristina asked me how I was faring at night school, and this gave me a chance to talk about my own troubles and the reason for my visit, to borrow a dress, shoes and stockings, if she would be kind enough to lend them to me.

'Certain, certain, you can have anything.' She paused and looked uneasily at her husband. 'I would not wish to anger your good Mother, though.'

'She need never know where I got the clothes from,' I assured her. 'I only need them for one afternoon. I'll think of another way of getting clothes for the job itself.' I had already thought of a possible source from which to obtain at least a dress, but not quickly enough for the interview.

Though Cristina might have qualms about offending my parents, her swaggering gallant of a husband had none. I think he had always resented my parents' supercilious attitude towards their neighbours and his pride had been hurt.

'Give them to her,' he ordered his wife, with such

a lordly gesture that the cat was disturbed from his shoulder and did a quick leap to the floor.

Cristina's eyebrows went up expressively and she shrugged. She got up from her chair, flicked her black shawl up round her shoulders, and said kindly to me, 'All right, my little one. Let us see what we can find.'

I bounced out of my chair, suddenly gay, and followed her. She had lent me old shoes on one or two earlier occasions, when she had observed that my running shoes were soaking wet; and long ago her gift of the Chariot had saved me the heavy task of carrying Edward everywhere when he was too young to walk.

Half an hour later, I glided through our back door, through the deserted kitchen and down the steps to the coal cellar, where I stowed away a brown paper bag containing shoes and stockings. On the inside of the cellar door, I hung a coat hanger which held a black dress with matching jacket shrouded in a piece of discarded curtaining.

'Who is there?' Father's voice came sharply from the living room.

'It's only me, Daddy.'

I opened the door and went in. The gaslight had been lit. The mantle was broken and the flame hissed and flickered over the comfortless room. The fire was out. Upstairs, I could hear the boys fighting in their bedroom. Presumably, Fiona, Avril and little Edward were asleep, since there seemed no sound from them.

'Where have you been?' Father's voice was freezing.

'To see Mrs Gomez. Where's Mummy?'

'She has gone down to Granby Street to buy a pair of stockings.' He flicked over a page of his book impatiently. 'You know I don't like you mixing with local people.'

I hung my head, but did not reply.

'If you have no homework to do, you had better go to bed.'

'Yes, Daddy.' I wondered if I should give him his usual good-night kiss, but he did not look up from his book, so I crept by him and went forlornly up to bed. I knew I had hurt him beyond forgiveness, and perhaps he really did not know how to cope with me.

Chapter thirteen

In the usual rush to get everybody off to school and themselves off to work, my parents had no time to discuss Miss Ferguson's visit with me. Mother gave me a shilling, as usual, to buy food, and two extra pennies to put in the gas meter. Father asked me to wash his second shirt ready for the next day, and suddenly Edward and I had the house to ourselves.

Greatly daring, I borrowed a large pair of scissors from a crippled Jewish lady who lived across the road. I was acquainted with her, because on cold winter Saturdays, Brian lit her fire for her and went over occasionally to make it up, since her religion demanded that she do no work on that day.

I stood in front of our piece of mirror in the kitchen window and hacked off the greasy rat's tails of hair until I was left with a short bob. I wished I had the family comb, but Mother had taken it to work with her. Then I attacked my nails, which were not very easy to cut with such big scissors, but finally they were snipped down to the flesh and that got rid of much of the dirt under them as well. Hair and body were then washed with a kettle of boiling water and a rag. I combed my hair with my fingers and smoothed it with the dirty towel.

My hands still looked awful. Then I remembered an old beauty trick of Grandma's. Feeling as if I was robbing Edward of a breakfast, I took a small pinch of oatmeal, damped the hands again and rubbed the oatmeal in hard. The hands emerged looking clean and much whiter than usual.

I put on the new pair of black woollen stockings which Cristina had lent me and found they would stay up fairly well if I twisted a piece of coal very tightly into the top of each.

How did one behave at an interview? I worried. What did one say? During the past three and a half years I had been practically cut off from all social contact. At an age when most middle-class girls would be being taught social graces by their school mistresses and their mothers, I had been walking the streets of Liverpool in rags, pushing a baby in a pram. Sometimes I was afraid I would forget how to speak properly. Only at night school did I ever get a chance to express myself. The lack of mental stimulation, the ever present lack of food, and the lack of fun and young friends had played havoc with an already shy personality – and I knew it.

As I scuttled round the shops in Granby Street with Edward in tow, and bought bread and potatoes and margarine, I silently said the General Confession and then the Lord's Prayer, turning towards the only help I knew. God received a rather wild collection of prayers that morning.

This mental exercise reminded me of Father's question as to whether I had approached the Anglican Fathers at the church about a job. The pressure Miss Ferguson had put on my parents *was* more than might normally have been expected. Perhaps Miss Ferguson had, after her tour of our house, consulted the priests. None of them had come to see us; but they had hooked Brian and Tony into the choir, so they knew we were High Anglicans. The idea that they might be trying to help me filled my romantic teenage heart with a kind of joy and lifted me for a while out of my wretchedness.

I fed the children when they came in for dinner and then dragged Fiona into the kitchen and confided to her the story of the job. Would she look after Edward for me, while I went for the interview?

'What if Mummy finds out?' she quavered, her eyes wide with misgiving.

'Oh, Fi, just take Avril to school and then slip back here. I'll be back ages before the boys or Mummy and Daddy come. They'll never know.'

'I'm scared, Helen. Teacher may be cross, too.'

'Look, I'll take all the blame. You can say I bullied you into it. They'll believe that. They'll blame me anyway.'

'Helen!'

She was very frightened and yet I had to have a baby-sitter for a couple of hours.

'Please, Fi, darling. Please.'

She shifted around unhappily and finally agreed.

While she took Avril to school, I put on the dress and the little jacket and then, as I squeezed a large acne spot on my chin and anxiously examined two more at the side of my nose, I agonised that she might not return. I peered anxiously at myself in the broken mirror. Behind the outgrown glasses my eyes were red with strain or pink eye. A further black rim round them from lack of food and rest did not add to my looks. I sighed, and ran to the window of the sitting room to see if Fiona was coming.

I had nearly given up hope, when she suddenly rounded the corner and dawdled down the street towards our house.

The walk down the hill to town was more painful than I had expected. The borrowed shoes pressed on the ragingly painful chilblains on my heels and toes. The wind blew the carefully arranged hair all over the place, and emphasised the need of a hat and a comb. Some of the euphoria which had sustained me evaporated, and was replaced by plain fear of the unknown.

To add to that, I had defied Father and Mother and I feared that I might be punished by God for it. He had said, Honour thy Father and thy Mother, and I presumed He meant what He said.

The closer I got to the city centre the more I quailed. And yet some stubborn instinct kept me going.

Without a watch, I did not know whether I was late or early and I hurried into the office building, which I had passed many times with Edward in the pram. It was a tall, Victorian structure with high, narrow windows looking out on a very busy side street.

The main floor was occupied by a tea-blending firm, and this confused me for a moment. A jolly, little woman with a steaming bowl of tea in her hand came to my rescue and directed me up the stone stairs.

I climbed and climbed. Half way up I had to stop.

Though I walked a lot in the fresh air, I was wasted from lack of food. A middle-aged lady in a green overall ran past me down the stairs without so much as a glance. A fat Irish woman in a black shawl and skirt panted her way upwards, muttering to herself. She gave me a sly grin as she passed.

Up I went again, and finally found the door mentioned by the lady with the tea bowl. I knocked and cautiously entered.

It was a big, ill-lit room with dusty yellow walls. There were several large tables, piled with files and papers, at which people sat engrossed in their work. In one corner stood a small table with a telephone on it. Behind the telephone stood a large wooden box with rows of knobs along its front. For a second, I imagined myself seated before the telephone trans-acting all kinds of important business.

At the back of the room stood rows of deep book-cases filled with files, and several girls in blue overalls were running about with stacks of brown folders in their arms. The only man in the room was a dark, saturnine person in a formal business suit, who sat at a large table writing in a big book. Two well-coiffured, smartly dressed ladies sat at the same table writing busily.

The gentleman looked up at my entrance.

'Yes?' he snapped.

Quivering with fright, I explained humbly over the bent heads of his lady helpers that I had come for an interview with the Secretary.

He sniffed, and gestured towards a young lady sitting before a typewriter. She smiled at me, took my name and made me sit down on a wooden chair with my back to the room.

While the typist knocked and went into an inner room, I thankfully regained my breath and tried surreptitiously to ease the agony of my feet inside the borrowed shoes.

When the typist returned to usher me into the inner room, I was sure I would faint with fright. However, she smiled very kindly at me, so I shuffled unhappily into the furnace.

At first I could not see anybody in the big, gloomy room. Then I realised that a woman, a tiny person, was seated at the desk by the window. I stood quaking just inside the door, after closing it silently behind me, until she looked up and took notice of me. She was plain to the point of ugliness, with greying hair combed neatly to her head. She had, however, a tremendous aura of authority, like all the ferocious head mistresses who had had me in their care rolled up into one powerful, scarifying personality.

While she examined me in the poor light from the overcast day, I stood with hands clenched together in front of me, awaiting the verdict.

Her voice when she spoke was cool and sibilant.

'You may sit down.'

Too scared to look at her again, I sat down on the edge of the chair by her desk. In answer to her questions, I said, 'Yes, madam,' or 'No, madam,' exactly as servants had done when addressed by Mother. I volunteered no information for which she did not explicitly ask. She had a file in front of her and occasionally she would flick over the papers in it with a long thin finger. It was apparent that she knew something of our family, and I presumed that Miss Ferguson had told her about us.

Finally, she said, without looking up, 'You may commence work next Monday. The hours are from nine to five-thirty on week days and nine until twelve-thirty on Saturdays. Two overalls will be provided for you to wear in the office and you will be expected to keep them clean. The salary is twelve shillings and sixpence a week.' She paused, and then said, after some consideration, 'The salary is payable monthly. However, in view of your family's circumstances I will arrange for you to be paid weekly.'

'Thank you, madam,' I said weakly. I'd got it! A real job!

'Report to Mr Ellis on Monday – in the outer office.'

'Yes, madam.'

I hesitated, uncertain whether I was dismissed or not. Part of me was mentally singing a Te Deum, part of me was so scared that for a moment or two I could not have moved.

'You may go now.' The voice was cold and disinterested, as if the mind behind it was already giving attention to other matters.

'Thank you very much, madam,' I said to a head already turned away from me.

But she had opened a Minute Book and was immersed in reading it, so I crept shakily to the door and went quietly out into the hustle of the general office.

I said, 'Thank you,' to the pretty typist, as I passed

her and she nodded back cheerfully, her fingers keeping up a constant tattoo on the typewriter before her.

Nobody else took any notice of me, so I slipped away, down the long staircases, like a warehouse cat. For a moment I shivered in the great pseudo-Gothic doorway, and then plunged into the crowd which thronged the pavement.

A blister had formed on top of a chilblain on my heel and it hurt sharply as I climbed the long hill towards home. The wind was so strong that it pushed and tousled me as if it had human hands. Fear of what lay ahead at home stole through me and sapped the strength from me; fear also that I would not be able to please my new employer. She had such a fearsome presence that I quailed at the memory of her.

She had asked me a number of questions, but she had not asked me the most important one. Had I any experience of using a telephone?

I had never spoken on a telephone, never even held a receiver in my hand. What it sounded like, how it worked, were both mysteries to me. The closest I had ever been to a phone was when I had occasionally stepped into a public phone box to press the 'B' button, to see if I could retrieve twopence forgotten by a caller who had failed to get his connection.

Chapter fourteen

It was nearly half past four when I hurried silently through the back door, slipping Cristina's jacket off as I ran.

The living-room door was slightly ajar, and I could hear the hurly-burly of the children at tea. Bless Fiona for making the tea!

In the cellar's cold blackness, smelling of coal and long departed cats, I carefully removed the borrowed dress, shoes and stockings, and pushed the latter back into the brown paper bag I had left down there. Naked, except for a torn pair of knickers, I ran up the stone steps and hung the precious dress and jacket on the inside of the cellar door. I hoped frantically that there was no coal dust on them.

Standing on the top step I slipped on my hopelessly short gym slip and a grey cardigan long since abandoned by Mother. Back in the kitchen, I stuffed my tortured feet into battered gym shoes; and I was back in character.

In the living room, Brian, Tony and Avril had left the table, and Brian was laying down the rules of a new game he had invented. The stairs would be a train, he would be the driver and the others the passengers. Without even looking at me, they ran into the hall, and I could hear them squabbling on the stairs about the details of the game and who would fall out first.

Edward was chewing a crust at the table, and I ruffled his hair playfully as I walked round him and sat down at the table opposite Fiona and Alan.

'How did you get on?' asked Alan. He nodded his blond head towards Fiona, and added, 'Fi told me.'

I told them of my success and they were jubilant. In spite of the family row the previous night Alan said he thought Mother and Father would relent. 'You've got to start some time,' he said firmly. 'It's only fair.'

It sounded as if he had given the matter some thought, and Fiona was equally enthusiastic, though it is doubtful if the poor, suppressed child ever really thought deeply about anything, other than what was happening to her at any given moment. Only when she unexpectedly burst into floods of tears did one know that deep inside the beautiful, doll-like creature was a human being who suffered dreadfully.

I had a misbegotten hope that my parents would be too tired to wage another battle. It was my mistake; they were never too tired to fight each other or lash out at me.

After they had eaten the scanty meal I had kept for them from the midday meal served to the children, and Mother was about to go upstairs to take off her work dress, I said in a carefully controlled voice that I would like to speak to them about Miss Ferguson's offer of a job.

They both looked at me with cold suspicion.

When I told them about the interview, they were

outraged. I was standing quite close to Father and he was so furious that he jumped up and struck me across the head. This stalled the hysterics I could feel rising inside me. They seemed more incensed about my disobedience than by the actual interview, and they took turns ranting about my general insubordination and lack of respect for their wishes.

I was myself very fatigued and was therefore quieter than usual, so that, unfueled, their fury began to trail off. Summoning up as much courage as I could muster, I announced that either I should be allowed to go to work or I would run away.

'What nonsense!' shouted Father. 'The police would bring you back, my girl. You are not even fifteen yet.'

I was frightened by his mention of the police, but I answered steadily, 'Not if I went to Grandma. If she lets my cousin work, she would let me go, too.'

Fortunately, they did not remember that I had no money for the ferry I would have to take to get to Grandma, and my threat sobered them.

Father laughed, and then said in a sad, dead voice, 'You would certainly not be welcome.'

Mother said savagely, 'The whole idea is absurd. You are needed at home.' She began to move towards the hall. 'Besides I could not possibly find the clothes for you. It's hard enough to keep myself dressed suitably.'

'I know, Mummy,' I replied quietly. 'And I've never ever asked you for clothes.' Then I added eagerly, 'But I have thought how I could get something to wear. If you would write to Mrs Fox, my friend Joan's mother, I think she would send me some. Joan and I were always much the same size – and she has wardrobes full of clothes.'

Mother tossed her head. 'I seem to remember your meeting Mrs Fox and her precious daughter in the town some time back, and that you told me they cut you dead.'

'They did, Mummy,' I agreed miserably. 'But when I thought about it some more, I think I understood how they felt. If they had stopped in Bold Street to speak to a ragamuffin like me, a crowd would have gathered. People would have thought I had stolen something off them or was begging.' I gave a shivery sigh. 'They did the right thing.'

'Humph,' said Mother, her hand on the knob of the hall door.

'I don't think you have ever written to Mrs Fox,' I went on persuasively. 'She's really very kind and generous.'

Father was looking me up and down, as if he had never seen my clothing before. He said suddenly, 'Helen needs clothes very badly by the look of her. That gym slip is hardly decent. It doesn't cover her properly.' He turned to Mother. 'Try to wheedle some clothes for her out of that Fox woman. She has more money than sense. It wouldn't hurt her to help her daughter's friend. I am sure Helen would feel much better if she had some decent garments.'

Perhaps he thought that, placated by some new clothes, I would be more amenable to being the family drudge.

'She might send some money, too,' I suggested.

Mother looked again at Father. He gave her the smallest affirmative nod.

'Very well,' said Mother coldly. 'I will write. We both need clothes.' Then in another burst of sudden anger, she turned to me. 'This doesn't mean that I have agreed to your going to work. I will not hear of it. You can't be spared.'

I ground my teeth, as I swallowed the angry retort I longed to make. Seething inwardly, I replied, 'Yes, Mother.'

The letter was written there and then, while Father watched; and the next few days were filled with anxiety. Creditors were visibly astonished when the front door was whipped open at their first knock, as I joyfully anticipated the coming of the postman. I listened sullenly to their upbraidings and then promised to tell Father all they threatened.

On the fourth day, the postal van arrived with two very large parcels. They were addressed to me, not to Mother.

I tore them open and went through the contents with wonderment. The dear woman had thought of everything; underwear, skirt, two blouses, shoes, gloves, overcoat, even a small, rather tired-looking handbag and a plain tam o'shanter for my head. There was a short letter wishing me well and mentioning that Joan was at a finishing school in Switzerland.

For a few moments, I touched and fondled the garments as if they were specially beloved possessions. I tried on the crumpled coat, a blouse and the skirt. They fitted reasonably well, though they were a little loose. I took them off reluctantly and folded everything into a pile. All the garments were so clean and sweet smelling, a gift from a world of bathrooms with soap and hot water, efficient laundries, and houses kept sparkling clean by maids armed with the newly-fashionable vacuum cleaner, tins of polish and bottles of disinfectant and liquid soap. As I stroked the little fur collar on the coat, I felt an overwhelming sadness, the sadness of someone bereaved who has come to terms with that bereavement but still at times mourns the loss.

I pulled myself together and picked up the string. Untangled, it would be strong enough to make a clothes-line across the kitchen on which to dry the children's clothes on wet days.

Gathering up the heap of clothes with the brown paper underneath them, I took them upstairs and laid them on Edward's and my bed. I hoped that the cleanliness of the clothing would deter the bugs from crawling on to them. When, later on, the fire would be lit for the children's homecoming I would heat our single flat iron and press the garments ready for Monday.

I dreaded the fighting yet before me; and I knew, from experience, that unless I was particularly adamant the parcel's contents would end up at the pawnbroker's.

Chapter fifteen

Edward and I went for our afternoon walk. It was raining slightly, so he rode in the Chariot and I put the ancient pram's hood up to protect him from the wet. Though the frame protruded through the rents in the cover, it still sheltered him fairly well. The rain slowly soaked my cardigan. I was used to it and did not care.

Our street was a straight line of terrace houses, once respectable working-class homes. Now the inhabitants were very mixed; and my father and a fireman who lived further down the street were the only two men in regular employment. Many of the homes had more than one family in them and were dirty and neglected. A few were very well kept; mended curtains arranged neatly on either side of the front window, with an aspidistra in a pottery bowl filling up the middle space, the window sill highly polished and the front step whitened.

Our beige curtains, as yet unpaid for, looked tidy behind windowpanes which I had washed with hot water and newspaper pads. Our front step, however, was littered with dried orange peel and cigarette ends flung there by our next door neighbours, whose front door abutted ours. They also spat on our step, as they sat on their own doorstep and smoked and read comic books. We never spoke to the man and wife and toddler who lived there. They would stare at us when we passed them, as if we were beings from another planet, and I suspect that they made ribald jokes at our stuffiness.

We walked the length of the long street, crossed Kingsley Road, which still had some shabby gentility about it, and continued on to Lodge Lane, where we spent a little while shop gazing, and I taught Edward the names of some of the household utensils exhibited in a chandlery shop.

The April clouds rolled away and the sun came out to make the rain-washed streets glitter with sudden cleanliness. When we neared home again, Edward said he wanted to walk. The pavement was no longer very wet, so I set him down on it and he ran ahead of me. I had made him a pair of bootees out of an old felt hat. They were stitched with wool from an unravelled sweater, and between two felt soles I had put a double layer of cardboard. I hoped the damp would not penetrate to his tiny feet.

Alice Davis was leaning against the doorjamb of her home as we came near, and she called to the small boy. He stopped and gave her one of his winning smiles. She stepped into the street and squatted down in front of him to talk baby talk to him. Then she ran back into the house and returned with a plain biscuit for him, which he snatched gladly out of her hand.

Though Alice was only about twenty-five years old, her face was lined and her smile practically toothless. She wore her black hair screwed into an unbecoming bun at the back of her head. Her blue-grey eyes were merry as she gently teased Edward.

I stopped to thank her for the biscuit and made Edward say, 'Thank you.'

'That's nothing,' she replied. Then she went on, 'That Mrs Ferguson come to see me about Edward. I said I'd take him. Did you get the job?' Her voice had the thick nasal accent of the born Liverpudlian.

'Yes,' I responded dully. 'I'm supposed to start on Monday.'

'Well, aren't you?' She looked me over disparagingly, and burst out, 'You're lucky, you are, to get a job.'

I nodded agreement. 'I know I am.' Then I thought suddenly that there is nothing like a *fait accompli*, so I said boldly, 'If you will look after Edward, I can start.'

'Oh, aye. I said I would. He's a little dear, he is.'

'I could pay you the ten shillings every Saturday afternoon when I come home from work. I think I would be paid on Fridays, but I am not certain. So I'll promise to bring it every Saturday.'

'Isn't that your Mam's business?'

I hesitated. I could not say that I doubted if Mother would pay regularly, so I said, 'We'll settle it between us. I'll bring Edward down every morning before I go to work, and Fiona can collect him when she gets back from school.'

Alice threw back her head and laughed. 'First few days you could bring him. After that he'll run up and down by himself, won't you, luv?' She bent down and chucked Edward under the chin. He swallowed the last of the biscuit and giggled and twisted away from her. ' 'Tis only a few doors away,' she added.

'If you think he'll be all right,' I said anxiously.

'Sure, he will. I'll see our door is open for him. And he can have a bit to eat with us at dinner time.'

'Thank you, Alice. I'm very grateful to you. See you on Monday morning – about eight o'clock.'

Alice bent down again and picked up Edward and nuzzled her face into his, laughing all the time. 'Yes. We'll have a proper nice time together.'

And with great relief I felt that she was right.

*

Clean out the grate, make the fire, lay clean newspaper on the table, cut the bread, make the tea, all with a stomach tight with apprehension. Would I ever know what it was like not to be frightened?

It was worse than I had expected.

Firstly, I had opened the parcel. Did I not realise that letters and parcels were opened by parents, regardless of how they were addressed? Furthermore, I had ironed the garments, thus accepting them without parental permission.

I had no right to speak to Alice. I had no right to say that I would begin work on Monday. Parents decided such a thing and they had decided that I should stay at home. It seemed to me that I had no rights at all, only a formidable list of obligations.

Cornered, terrified rats turn and attack. Some human beings, however, have less courage, and I was ready to give in, when help came suddenly from an unexpected quarter.

Fiona said in a quivering voice, 'I can make the tea and take care of Edward and Avril till you come home,

Mummy. And I can help to put them to bed. I could even do the shopping if you gave me a list.'

It must have cost her dearly to speak up on my behalf. It came as a surprise to me that she should love me enough to do so. I gave love but I did not expect anything in return. I had always protected her as much as I could from hunger and cold and jeering local boys and girls, helped her with her homework because she had great difficulty in learning, and frankly admired her because she had such a sweet temperament. And now, on my behalf, the gentle creature was laying herself open to our parents' bitter censure. I was moved beyond words and was still gaping at her, when Alan put down his toast and said, 'I don't mind giving a hand as well.'

Alan and I had always got along very well, once I had recovered from the infant jealousy which his birth had engendered; and I was grateful for his intercession. Mother loved her sons and would listen to him.

Alan was saying stoutly that all girls went to work now. A lady from the employment exchange had come to the school to counsel them about work, and she had interviewed the girls as well as the boys. So it must be so.

Though Father was still trembling with rage, I could see he was listening to Alan's remarks. Mother started to cry and say that she could not manage, and I felt dreadful, because the ultimate responsibility for all of us rested on her shoulders. She was not idle after returning from work; she would rest for a little while and then spend some time with Edward and

Avril. While I was at night school, she would check the children's clothes after they had gone to bed and sometimes did part of the washing and ironing. She was not in the best of health, and her tears racked me.

Fiona and Alan were, however, arguing in a soothing way that the family was big enough and each of them old enough to make it possible for me to be spared.

Father got up suddenly and swung out of the room. I saw him take his trilby hat off the hall peg and clap it down on his head. Without a word, he lifted the latch of the front door and went out into the ill-lit street. I knew from experience that when he came back he would smell of beer and would be amiably jocular with all of us.

As he went, Mother blew her nose quickly, and then shouted after him, 'You can't face anything, can you? Must you always waste money on drink?'

He did not reply. Shell-shocked, war weary, he had been ill enough himself to draw a full army pension for several years after serving in Russia. Probably his nerves screamed for sedation, and his comfortless home and unruly family made the pain unbearable.

Fiona got up and put her arms round Mother's neck. 'Don't cry, Mummy. If Helen goes to work, she's so clever she'll soon earn lots and lots. And then you will be able to stay at home and not have to work any more.'

Fiona's and Alan's advocacy gave me a little courage again. I was so terribly unhappy myself that I felt I could not go on as I had been doing; something had to give. Unlike Fiona, I was quite sure that the last thing Mother wanted was to be at home with her family all day; yet my needs deserved consideration, too.

'Let us try, Mummy,' I begged. 'I should get more money after a little while and it would help.'

But Mother was still flaming with wrath. She pushed Fiona away, bounced out of her chair and shook her finger at me. 'You are talking rubbish. You are disobedient and ungrateful. You haven't even matriculated. You are unskilled in anything.'

I fired up immediately, 'And whose fault is that?'

Mother nearly choked. She slapped me across the face. 'I never heard such impudence,' she screamed.

I backed away from her, snatched up my night school books from the mantelpiece, and tried not to scream back, as I said, 'I don't care. I'm going to work on Monday. Otherwise, I am going to Granny's – so you won't have my help anyway.'

Mother had been a very beautiful woman. Convulsed with rage, she looked like an infuriated witch, and I was terrified.

'Go!' she yelled at me. 'All right. Go to work! You will soon discover that the world is a very cruel place and you will long to be at home again. Get out of my sight.'

By this time all the children were bellowing like frightened cows. Fiona and Avril clung to Mother, crying, 'Don't, Mummy, don't.' Brian, Tony and Edward were all in noisy tears. Only Alan sat tearless; he yelled, 'I don't know why everybody had to make such a row!'

I backed through the door. Then turned and followed Father into the night.

Mother did not need to tell me that the world outside was a cruel place. I knew that already. But faintly, faintly on the horizon it had its rays of hope.

Chapter sixteen

'Mr Ellis,' I whispered shyly, 'I am the new telephone girl.'

Four other girls in the room paused in their work to stare at me, while Mr Ellis put down his pen carefully on his desk and looked up at me. He frowned at what he saw.

'Humph. You are?' He took out his handkerchief and held it to his nose. I heard a girl giggle.

I lowered my eyes. I knew I looked awful. Joan's skirt and blouse hung on me. My rough-cut hair could have served as a mop. Both feet throbbed with the pain of blisters rubbed on tender chilblains, and I was biting my lips as I endured the misery of it. Over me lay the smell of poverty, of a body poorly washed, clothes unaired, foul breath and fatigue.

The man before me was thin and dark-visaged, with the same air of nervous tension as Father had. He called to a girl sitting in front of the telephone switchboard.

'Miss Finch, show t' girl what to do.'

He gestured towards the switchboard with his pen, as he picked it up, so I silently went over to Miss Finch. While I stood awkwardly beside her, I could see out of the corner of my eye, two other girls sniggering behind their hands as they watched.

Miss Finch answered the telephone in a thick

Liverpool accent. In between calls, without preamble, she explained to me that people wishing to apply to the Charity for help entered through the basement, where there was a waiting room. A girl took their names and telephoned them up to the room we were in. The switchboard operator wrote them down and handed the slips of paper to the filing clerks. The applicant's file, if any, was then sent down to the Interviewing Floor directly below us, where there was another waiting room.

The applicant was then sent upstairs, past the Tea Blending Company on the main floor, to be united with his file. At this point, a senior staff member inquired what he had come about, and he was then seated in the second waiting room. He was finally interviewed in a side room. It was a long, slow process for the applicants.

Miss Finch was a black-haired, rosy-cheeked girl, who seemed to resent me very much. She told me she was the office girl and was filling in on the switch-board until I could take over. I presumed that she had not won promotion to the job of telephonist because of her bad accent.

'Names beginning A to J go to Dorothy Evans; K to Z to Phyllis over there.' She got up and handed me the phone. 'You take the next call from the basement.'

Gingerly, I lifted the receiver to my ear, while Miss Finch moved the appropriate switches. A garbled rattle came through the receiver. I could not interpret it. In a panic, I handed the instrument back to Miss Finch, who hastily jotted down a name on her pad.

'What's the matter?' she asked impatiently, as she handed me the slip. 'Give this to Phyllis Barker.' When I hesitated uncertainly, she hissed, 'Over there. Be quick.'

Phyllis snatched the slip out of my hand, quickly jumped up and vanished down her aisle of files. Her high-heeled patent leather shoes flashed, as she moved.

'How do you answer the phone and deliver the names to the filing clerks at the same time?' I whispered to Miss Finch.

Miss Finch made a wry face. 'You run,' she whispered back. 'Everybody runs.'

She was right. The filing clerks, the telephonists, the disembodied voice in the basement, the whimpering nervous girl who served in the Cash Department next door, Miss Finch herself as she made tea and delivered letters, all ran. Like convicts, at the double, they scuttled upstairs and downstairs, scurrying in and out of offices to look for files or deliver messages, running, running, running. Sometimes, I almost expected them to take wing, like one does in nightmares. They were not allowed to use the lift, because the charity was short of money and it was necessary to keep the electricity bill to a minimum.

Miss Finch left me to manage the telephone alone for a few minutes. She had to sort some letters into a round for hand delivery and did this at another table. In seconds, the awesome Presence who had interviewed me and had given me the job, shuffled out of her room, to inquire of Miss Danson, her secretary, why she had found herself speaking to her own basement when she wanted to speak to the Public Assistance Committee two miles away.

Miss Danson murmured about the new girl just starting and eased her back into her room, while Mr Ellis barked at both Miss Finch and me to be more careful.

It was a dreadful morning, during which I managed to create telephonic chaos. I could hardly hear what was said. I had no idea of the names of the other staff or where they were to be found. I had no list of commonly required outside numbers and had to look each of them up in the telephone book. And, quickly enough, I realised from Miss Finch's manner that she did not feel it was in her interest to help me to make a success of the job.

I was left alone, while Miss Finch went to make the office's morning tea, and I called almost tearfully to Phyllis to come to help me sort the switchboard out.

'Not Phyllis, Miss Forrester,' roared Mr Ellis, behind me, 'Miss Barker, if you please.' He paused, while I sat paralysed with fright, and then said, 'Can't you speak quieter? I can't stand that la-dee-da accent.'

'Yes, sir,' I whispered, as Phyllis Barker kindly came to my aid.

I realised suddenly that, except for Mr Ellis, everyone in the room whispered. And nobody laughed. Not one girl, except Miss Barker, had even smiled at me yet. The constant tattoo of the type-writer of the Presence's secretary, the buzz of the telephone switchboard, the flutter of paper and the steady hiss of whispers made up the noises in the room.

Miss Finch told me my lunch hour would be from

one-thirty to two-thirty, and the morning seemed endless. She dumped a cup of tea in front of me with a biscuit tucked in the saucer, and I ate and drank eagerly. In a quiet moment Miss Barker found me a list of commonly-used telephone numbers and I tried to master it. The names and figures danced in front of me. I needed badly a list of the names of the staff and their numbers on the switchboard, so that I could connect incoming calls to the correct extension; and when Miss Finch returned to assist me, I asked her for this.

She shrugged and said I did not need a list. I would soon learn the names. In the meantime, outraged voices on every extension phone sibilantly rebuked me. It was a nightmare.

At twelve o'clock, the basement waiting room closed and there were no more names to write down and deliver to the filing clerks. This gave me more time to deal with other calls and contemplate more quietly the hateful, buzzing board.

Just before lunch time, a thin waif of a girl wearing large horn-rimmed glasses came out of a door on the other side of the room.

With an apprehensive glance at Mr Ellis, she crept over to me and said in an almost inaudible voice, 'The Cashier would like to see you during your lunch hour.' She sniffed, and I saw that she had been crying. Her nose was red and her eyes heavy with tears. It looked as if she had been in even more trouble than I had.

'The Cash Department is over there,' she added, pointing to the room from which she had come.

I smiled up at her. 'Thanks. I'll come.'

She managed a glimmer of a smile back and then fled across the room and through the door she had pointed out to me.

Fear of what lay in wait in the Cash Department was added to my fear of the telephone.

*

I knocked at the Cash Department door and a female voice snapped, 'Come in.'

I entered. The room was partly divided by a frosted glass screen and at first appeared to be empty. I paused.

'Well?' snapped the same voice again, from behind the glass screen.

I approached cautiously.

Behind the screen, at a littered desk, sat a small, grey-haired woman. She looked at me almost belligerently. 'What do you want?'

'You sent for me, Madam. I am Helen Forrester.'

'Hmm.' She looked me up and down, and her nose wrinkled in distaste.

She turned round and took two folded blue garments from a shelf behind her. These she almost threw into my arms.

'Your overalls. You will wear them at all times in the office and will keep them clean.'

'Yes, madam.'

'You will be paid on Friday afternoons. Such a nuisance to have to pay a single member of the staff on a weekly basis. What is your full name and address? And age?'

I told her.

'Very well. You can go.' She turned back to her desk, and I tiptoed out, past two empty desks where presumably the weepy girl and another person worked.

The general office was empty, except for an elderly lady in a pretty grey dress who was manning the telephone. She nodded to me as I went out.

I went up to the cloakroom on the top floor of the building. This had been shown to me when I arrived, by a hurrying lady in a green overall whom I had met on the stairs. I laid the two blue overalls on the floor under the hook where I had hung my coat, and wondered what to do. There was nobody about and the silence seemed unearthly. I began to cry, my head pressed against my coat.

I had no money to buy lunch, and there had been no bread left after breakfast to bring with me. Both parents had left me severely alone, to get myself ready for work and Edward ready to go to Alice's. Feeling like a pariah, I had taken the cheerful little boy to his new friend's and he had stayed with her without a murmur, and then I had walked to work.

There was no doubt in my mind that my parents were united in their attitude that I should find going to work so difficult that I would eventually be thankful to return to housekeeping.

At the memory of their stony faces, I felt suddenly weak. I moved to the wash basin and clung to it, as my legs began to give under me. Wild colours flashed before my eyes and I felt myself sinking into oblivion. I knew from experience that I rarely passed out completely, so I clung to the wash basin until the world stopped swimming about.

I cupped my hand under the cold tap and drank some water, slurping it up and splashing my face. Greatly daring, I decided to have a wash. My face was soaped as it had never been soaped in the past three years. I rinsed and rinsed in gorgeous hot water, then dried myself on the spotlessly clean roller towel.

The light was poor, but in the mirror I could see green eyes with black rings round them, peering out of a face dead white, except where it was blotched with acne. Short eyelashes hardly showed on the reddened eyelids. Smooth eyebrows looked very black below a rough fringe of brown hair. I grinned ruefully at myself. The teeth thus exposed looked good – the cavities at the back did not show.

The wash had done me good and, as nobody disturbed me, I washed my glasses, dried them on the towel and put them on. The face in the mirror came into sharper focus, and I could see again how defeatingly plain I was. How I longed for a perfectly straight nose, like Fiona's, instead of the high-bridged, haughty-looking Forrester nose.

Without a watch I did not know the time. Meanwhile, I needed to sit down, and there was no chair in the cloakroom.

Hesitantly, I looked along the line of blue overalls hung neatly on their owners' hooks, and saw beyond them a door leading off the cloakroom.

Very quietly, I approached the door and opened it.

I was in a small passage. To my left, an open door revealed a neat kitchenette. It had a big window and was bright with light. Another closed door faced me. When I turned its handle, it gave a sharp click.

'Hello. Come in,' said a soft feminine voice very cheerfully.

Chapter seventeen

Embarrassed that I had disturbed someone, I swung the door wide and stood dithering on the threshold of a small room that seemed packed with furniture bathed in dazzling sunlight. Light from a skylight poured down onto the burnished brown head of a thin woman, about twenty-five years of age, who was seated facing me behind one of the three typists' desks crowding the room. She had an open paperback in one hand and was eating a sandwich. As she looked up at me from her book, her long, narrow face radiated good humour. She had a beautiful pink and white skin, delicately accentuated by good make-up, and light, almost catlike brown eyes gazed at me through very large horn-rimmed glasses.

'Hello, come in,' she said, as she put her book down on top of her typewriter. 'What brings you here? You must be the new telephonist.'

'Yes,' I replied. 'I am sorry to intrude. I was looking for somewhere to sit down.'

'Oh, take Miss Short's chair for a while. She won't mind.' She pointed to a swivel chair by another typist's desk. 'Like a sandwich?'

'Thank you.'

I willed myself not to snatch from the proffered square of greaseproof paper. Carefully, I took the tiny triangle and made myself eat it in several delicate, polite bites, when I really longed to bolt it down. It was a cucumber sandwich and reminded me poignantly of long ago afternoon teas. The other girl ate the two remaining sandwiches and tossed the empty wrapping into the wastepaper basket. She insisted on my sharing a small piece of fruit cake with her.

I smiled at her, as I ate the cake, and asked, 'Are you somebody's secretary?'

'No.' She laughed. 'I'm just one of the also-rans. I do any typing jobs they want.'

'Could I ask your name?' I queried. 'I don't know the names of any of the staff, except some of the filing clerks, and it is terribly difficult when answering the phone.'

'Well, I'm Miriam Enns. And Miss Short and Miss Brown work up here. Miss Short is the Head Typist. Then Miss Danson in the Filing Department is the secretary to Miss MacAdam, who runs the place. You probably saw her when you applied for the job.'

'I did.' Then I added, without thinking, 'The Presence.'

'The what?' Miriam chuckled delightedly. 'That's lovely.'

I blushed, and smiled nervously. Then I said, 'Well, she seemed like a Presence.'

'You are right. She's a great lady and she works very hard, though she is so frail.' She swung round on her chair, took a piece of paper out of her stationery stand and put it into her typewriter. 'I'll make you a list of the staff – it won't take a minute. I don't know the numbers of their phones on the switchboard, but I can tell you which floor they are on.'

She rattled away on the machine, while I sat quietly watching her. She seemed to me the nicest person I had met for a very long time, and as I watched her long, slender fingers flash over the keyboard, a new emotion welled up in me, a great desire to give and receive friendship.

'That Ellis man should have seen that you got a list like this,' she said irritably, as she whipped the paper from the roller and handed it to me.

'Thanks,' I said happily, as I carefully folded the paper up. 'Is he the only man on the staff?'

'No, there is one more. But I think Ellis finds it hard in a sea of women.'

I did not venture a comment. I was a bit afraid of Mr Ellis, who did not approve of la-dee-da accents.

'Have you got an overall yet?' asked Miriam. She took a packet of cigarettes out of her own blue overall pocket, struck a match from a box on her desk and lit up.

'Yes.'

'Better put it on. We lowly types wear blue ones. Senior staff – the social workers – wear green ones.'

I nodded agreement.

There was the sound of the cloakroom door being opened and slammed, and running feet.

Miriam glanced at her wrist watch. 'It's twenty-five past,' she said. 'Better put on your overall and go downstairs – or Ellis will be after your blood.'

I jumped up. I felt a lot better.

'Thank you for your help,' I said warmly, looking down at the pixie face of my new friend.

Miriam had the same type of wide, red-lipped

mouth as Fiona had, and she smiled broadly up at me. 'When you get desperate, come up here,' she advised. Her smile became a yawn and she took off her glasses and rubbed her merry, brown eyes with her knuckles.

'I'd love to,' I assured her enthusiastically.

'Shut the door as you go out. Miss Short doesn't like it left open.'

Obediently I closed the door after me. I paused in the passage outside, my hand still on the door knob, feeling again the warm friendliness of the girl in the typing room. For the first time since arriving in Liverpool, I had talked with someone fairly young, who spoke as I did and treated me as an equal.

Chapter eighteen

The aim of the organisation in which I found myself was to make the poor aware of the many charities available to help them; to counsel; to provide a little legal aid given voluntarily by a few city lawyers; and to disburse, in the most constructive way, funds donated to the organisation itself. The senior staff provided a friendly ear for sorrows to be poured into, and sympathetic visitors to the sick and other house-bound people; they tried also to aid the elderly and the many despairing mothers who, under impossible circumstances, struggled to make ends meet. Though they were not well paid, all the staff had shining neatly combed hair, clear skins and well-fed bodies. Their clothes were fresh looking and everything matched, as was the fashion. I was thankful to be shrouded in an overall.

Filled with dismay at my lack of knowledge, not only of the telephone, but of the myriad of social nuances, the courtesies, of this new world, I struggled on to the end of the day. The other girls, with a hasty 'good-night' ran for their trams, and I trudged slowly home, head bent against a blustery wind. A cup of tea brought to me during the afternoon had reduced the pangs of hunger, but I felt very weak. Night school would begin at seven o'clock, and I wondered how I would manage to get there in time.

I badly needed food, warmth, and a little comforting encouragement that tomorrow I would do better.

When I slowly opened the door of the living room, I saw that Father was seated in the old easy chair, deep in a book. I wondered why he was not reading in the front room, but decided it was probably too cold for him in there. Alan, his blond cowlick swinging over his forehead, was seated on a small upturned oil drum by the fire. His head was bent over an exercise book while he did his homework.

Brian, Tony and Avril were sailing an imaginary ship across the floor. Brian was shouting to his bosun, Tony, 'Ahoy there, Bill. Belay there.' And then to Avril, he called, 'Hard astarboard, you lazy landlubber.' And Avril laboriously turned a huge, imaginary wheel. They were so absorbed in the game that they did not reply when I said, 'Hello, children.'

'Hello, Daddy. Hello, Alan.'

They both looked up from their occupations and nodded acknowledgment in a vague, guarded way, then went back to their reading. Only Baby Edward, who was whining steadily, toddled towards me, to put his arms round my legs. I picked him up and hugged him, in an effort to assuage the terrible sense of emptiness within me, and carried him into the kitchen from which came the clatter of dishes.

Fiona was filling the sooty, tin kettle from the tap, and she half-turned and smiled at me timorously in the flickering light of the candle on the draining board. Beside her, Mother was emptying teacups into the soapstone sink. She said, 'Oh, you've come. have you? You *are* late.'

I stroked the back of Edward's scurfy head, as I answered, 'It took a long time to walk home.'

I looked uneasily at both of them. I sensed that something had gone wrong. I could almost smell it. And it was my fault. I could see it in Mother's stiffened back and frozen look as she swung round to the back door, teapot in hand, to empty the leaves down the outside drain.

'Down?' requested Edward, and very slowly I slid him on to the worn tiles, my eyes on Fiona, in the hope that she would give me a hint while Mother's back was turned. Her eyebrows went up and she gave an almost imperceptible shrug. She seemed scared, and turned hastily back to the kettle, which was running over with water.

Mother clicked her tongue when she saw the overflow.

'Fiona, you stupid girl. Empty some of it out. Put the lid on and then put it on the fire.'

Obediently, Fiona did this and then slid past me into the living room, to put the kettle on to heat. Edward toddled after her, and I could hear him saying to Brian, 'Me, too. I want to play.'

I was left to face Mother.

'You had better get yourself something to eat,' she said frigidly.

I had begun to tremble. It started in my legs and worked its way up, until all of me seemed to be shaking. Was nobody interested in what had happened to me? Surely, normal curiosity would have brought a question or two. Whatever had happened in my absence must indeed have been terrible to blot out all remembrance that this had been my first day at work. I waited for the blow to fall, as I whispered, 'Yes. I am very hungry.'

I turned to the deal kitchen table upon which lay half a loaf of bread and a very misused-looking pat of margarine sitting on its wrapping paper. 'Can I make some tea?'

'Yes,' replied Mother. 'The milk is still on the table. That's all the bread we've got.' She went swiftly into the living room and I heard her go through to the front hall.

I closed my eyes, as if by shutting out the world, I might persuade the trembling to cease. I wanted to seize the spongy piece of white bread, tear it apart and stuff it in my mouth and gobble it down. I could have eaten the margarine in big, revolting chunks. But Mother's words had gone into me like a sharp hat pin. What she had really said was, 'You should not eat anything. If you do, the children will not have any breakfast.'

But I had to eat. So I took up the knife and very carefully, because my hands were so unsteady, I cut a slice off the loaf and put some margarine on it. Despite a throat tight with misery, I ate it, standing there, staring down at the grey surface of the table.

When I went into the living room to ask Fiona for some water from her kettle in order to make a cup of tea, she was standing aimlessly watching the game of ships. I touched her shoulder. She jumped and turned towards me, her expression unaccountably defensive as if she expected to be struck. I saw that she had been crying.

At my request, she took the singing kettle off the fire and brought it into the ill-lit kitchen.

I asked in a low voice, as I put a pinch of tea into a cup and poured water on to it. 'What's up, Fi? What has happened?'

She looked suddenly as if she would burst into tears again, and my trembling increased. Her usually red lips looked almost bloodless and she pushed her straight brown hair back from her face with hands that shook. She whispered dismally, 'Oh, Helen. I did a terrible thing. Mother and Father are furious. And they're awfully cross with you, too, for not being here . . .'

In my opinion, Fiona never did anything wrong, so probably it was my fault. As she started to cry, I quickly reviewed the family. Everybody seemed well; nobody appeared to have been hurt.

Fiona was nearly as tall as me, and I put my arm round her lanky frame. 'What is it, Fi?' I asked, through chattering teeth. But she just put her head on my shoulder and cried harder, long, slow sobs, silent like mine usually were, but sobs that seemed to be wrenched out of the innermost depths of her. My own despair was forgotten in the new fear of what had happened to upset her so much.

'What is it, Fi?' I implored again.

She gave a huge snuffle and began to mutter into my ear.

'Well, some men came with a big van – and they hammered on the front door until I simply had to answer. And they said they had come to collect the furniture because we were behind in our payments.

And both Mummy and Daddy are so angry because I let them in and they took it.' She lifted her face towards mine, and then said desperately, 'But I couldn't help it, Helen. They were so big – and one of them put his foot in the door so that I couldn't slam it shut. I was so scared, Helen.' And she began another flood of tears.

'They really took it away?'

'Yes. The front room is empty.'

I began to chuckle quietly, so as not to draw Daddy's attention.

'It's nothing to laugh about, Helen,' Fiona whispered forcefully. 'It was terrible.'

'There, now, Fi. Don't cry. Don't you see? We don't have to pay for it any more. That is five more shillings a week in the house. It's glorious. Think, five shillings will buy at least twenty more loaves a week. That's two loaves a week each. Cheer up, love.'

Fiona wiped her eyes with the back of her hand.

'Oh, no,' she said harshly, her voice heavy with sarcasm. 'No such luck. Father says we have to go on paying, whether we have the furniture or not. It's in the agreement.'

My trembling ceased entirely at this sudden revelation. I looked at her unbelievingly.

'Pay for what we haven't got? What nonsense.'

In my innocence, I knew nothing of hire purchase agreements or how they were abused by some companies doing business in the city. Many, many people were caught up in this vicious system, and many of them paid for years, because they either failed to read the small print in the agreements they signed or they did not understand the jargon in which they were couched. There were, of course, many reputable companies who stood by the spirit as well as the letter of their agreements. But my parents had apparently fallen victim to the blandishments of some salesman who was, perhaps, himself desperate for the commission he would get on the sale.

'We do, Helen. We have to pay.'

I looked wildly round me, for someone or something on which to vent my frustration.

'Where was Alan when all this happened?' I asked savagely. 'Couldn't he have helped you keep the door shut?'

'He wasn't home from school. It wasn't his fault. I left Avril with him and ran on ahead. I wanted to have the tea ready for you when you came home.' She looked piteously at me and sobbed again.

'Never mind, Fi, dear. You did your very best. Don't cry any more. I have to go to night school. And I must get Edward and Avril off to bed.'

I patted her on the shoulder, took a large breath and strode into the living room. 'Bybyes time, darling,' I said to Edward, and with a laugh swept him up off the imaginary ship. A few minutes later, I forcibly dragged Avril away from the game to have her face, hands and knees hastily wiped before popping her into bed. Brian and Tony began to quarrel as to who should be thrown overboard to the sharks. Father told them irritably to get ready for bed, and Alan asked equally irritably if he would ever be allowed to do his homework in peace.

I had brought my books down from the bedroom

after hearing recalcitrant Avril's prayers, and now I picked them up and ran out through the back door. Fiona was washing her face under the tap and I shouted goodbye to her as I went by.

Two quiet, orderly hours in school restored me.

Chapter nineteen

The next morning, a few minutes after I arrived, breathless and hungry, the Presence sent for me. I was still very upset from the bitter recriminations of my parents, which had burst forth from both of them as they rushed between living room and kitchen getting themselves washed and dressed for work. Mother had gone out the previous evening to the pawnbroker and had pawned all the clothes which Mrs Fox had sent, except what I was wearing, and this had added to my distress. It was a very miserable and frightened young girl who crept into the Presence's office, and stood humbly waiting for her to speak.

She looked up from her desk and in a few crisp, sharp words she dismissed me for inefficiency. She gave me a week's notice.

My small world, my new hopes, shattered round me. It was as if they fell like tinkling glass from a broken window, leaving me naked to a winter wind.

As I stood dumbly staring at her without any idea of what I should do, she turned the pages of a file on the desk in front of her. Gradually my eyes focused on her long, shrivelled fingers and following the line of them, I saw that the file was marked 'Forrester', in large capital letters.

In the silence, the significance of the file slowly dawned upon me. At some point, my parents must have applied to my employers for help. And a file on our family must have been sitting on the shelves in the outer office, available for all the girls to read. I felt so mortified at the idea of a social worker's report on our poverty-stricken home being read by the other girls, that I wondered how I would manage to face them during the week's notice the Presence had just served on me.

She was speaking again. 'Miss Finch will be promoted to telephonist. I am prepared to give you another chance as office girl in her place. Her salary is ten shillings a week.'

Reprieve! I snapped up the offer.

Ten shillings would pay Alice. And people got rises in pay, didn't they? Perhaps I would, if I could last out long enough.

She lifted the telephone receiver. 'I will speak to Mr Ellis. Report to him.' She gave me a grim, small smile of dismissal, and I crept out of the room. Her manner was cool and distant, and yet I felt that, amid the many worries of her day, she had tried to help me.

I did not look at any of the other girls, as with eyes downcast I went over to Mr Ellis's desk and stood by him, waiting to be noticed. He was saying, 'Yes, yes. I understand,' down the telephone. Finally he hung up the telephone receiver, and swivelled round towards me.

'That's a proper mess now, isn't it?' he barked.

I hung my head and said nothing.

While I waited, crestfallen, he reorganised his staff, so that Miss Finch could spend the day showing me what to do. Then I was borne off by a naturally triumphant Miss Finch to hurry into our outdoor clothes again.

All letters addressed to destinations within approximately one mile of the office were delivered by hand, as were urgent ones to more distant addresses. One of the sights of the city was the vast number of small office boys and girls trotting about, delivering letters. Their wages were cheaper than the cost of postage.

I knew the city well and soon sorted the letters into a round, and Miss Finch and I set out together. In and out of lawyers' offices, shipping offices and shops we tramped. There was even a letter for the Liverpool Playhouse, which we excitedly delivered at the stage door, hoping against hope that we might catch a glimpse of one of the actors. But we were disappointed. A joking, cheerful doorman took the missive from us.

Mary warned me that the lift men in some of the buildings were not to be trusted, and several times she insisted that we walked up the stairs, once as far as the sixth floor.

I did not understand the import of her warning until the next day, when I did the round on my own. Two men pawed me, while with one hand they pulled the rope that carried the lift upwards. I shrank into the far corner where I could not be reached. This did not deter one of them who, with a grin, stopped the lift at a deserted top floor and pinned me into the corner.

Instinctively I screamed at the top of my voice, and pushed away the exploring hands with all the force I could command. The letters scattered over the floor of the lift. I was panic-stricken, though I could not have said what I was frightened of.

When I shrieked the man let go of me. He turned and angrily flung open the iron gates, and told me to get out and walk. He picked up the letters and threw them after me, as I shot past him onto the landing. I snatched up the letters and scampered down the staircase to the floor I needed. I was sickened, as he slowly followed me down in the lift whispering obscenities which I had previously only come across scribbled on the walls of public lavatories and had never quite understood. His leering face, seen through the iron gates as I passed them on my way down, haunted my nightmares for several days.

This was the first time that anyone had made a sexual advance to me, and, since I did not really understand what the threat to me was, I was filled with nameless terrors for a long time, and learned to run upstairs like a rabbit. Practically all the novels I read ended with a first kiss and I imagined that a happy marriage was a life of gentle tenderness. That there was a physical side to it was unknown to me. I had washed my brothers often enough to know that there was a difference between boys and girls, and Edith had always washed us and dressed us in front of each other, so it all seemed perfectly natural, as did the fact that elm trees and oak trees had different types of leaves.

I had once watched a bull amongst a herd of cows and understood from the cowman that they were making calves. I vaguely understood that babies were carried in their mothers' stomachs, because some of my brothers and sisters had been born at home; and I had picked up from scurrying maids a little of what was happening, but how the baby got there was unknown to me and I presumed that its beginning was spontaneous, though I gave it surprisingly little thought. I knew I was too plain for marriage so would not be having any babies anyway.

During the past two years, while I had been developing into a woman, I had been entirely cut off from the speculative gossip of young girls. Mother had not seen fit to explain anything to me or to warn me of any danger to myself. Yet I sensed now a real physical danger and I gave a wide berth to all liftmen and commissionaires.

When Miss Finch and I returned to the office, we dashed up the stairs to the kitchen to make the morning tea. A tray was spread for the Presence, kettles were filled and cups and saucers were assembled on other trays. A box of biscuits was opened and a biscuit put on every saucer.

While Miss Finch delivered tea to the Presence and to the people working on the same floor as the Filing Department, I ran down the innumerable stone stairs to the basement, carefully balancing in one hand a cup of tea for Miss Lester, who took the names of the clients when they first entered.

The stench in the badly-ventilated cellar room was appalling, as I handed the cup of tea to the blue-clad girl seated at a tiny table facing the clients. She thanked me, while about twenty pairs of eyes watched silently. I paused by the table, expecting Miss Lester to make some light remark or other. Gossiping, however, was a major sin in the eyes of Mr Ellis, so she said nothing.

I looked out over the clients and they stared back at me. There were fat women in black shawls, black skirts and white aprons. They were Liverpool Irish, I knew. Once or twice, while sitting in the park watching the children play, I had spoken to such women shyly about their children, and found them kind and responsive. Some of them still had the high colour of country women, but most of them looked white and drained of strength.

There were also a few women in coats and hats, shabby and grey. A number of men in stained working clothes sat quietly, with their cloth caps held neatly on their laps. One or two children fidgeted fretfully on the wooden benches or sat on the coconut matting which covered the stone floor. Low watt bulbs cast a poor light over the well-ordered crowd.

Perhaps it was their quietness, their resignation to the long wait for attention, which was most depressing. They seemed people who had lost all hope, and my heart went out to them. I understood why they smelled, the exhaustion which made them so very quiet. The organisation, I guesssd correctly, had not enough money to enable them to offer their clients a cup of tea. Thoughtfully I stole back up the stairs to the kitchen.

'You were a long time,' complained Miss Finch impatiently. 'Take this tray down to the first floor. Give each of the interviewers a cup – and don't forget the volunteer at the centre table.'

I took the heavy tray of filled cups and carried it

carefully down to the first floor. Balancing it on one hand, I pushed the landing door to open it. A youth as thin as a broomstick held it open for me as I passed through. I saw his face light up at the sight of the tea tray, and I felt dreadful because I could not give him a cup.

It was another waiting room which smelled equally badly and was equally gloomy. There was only one light hanging above a centre table round which a screen had been set. A well-dressed lady sat at the table, a neat row of files before her. At the side of the table on a wooden chair sat an ancient bundle of bones hunched under a thick blanket shawl. Her tiny face, dark from lack of washing, peered anxiously out from the shawl, like a mouse peeping out of its hole. Little hands clutching the shawl across her breast were equally mouselike. She watched me put a cup of tea down by the voluntary worker, and I felt for a second the old woman's clemmed stomach, the agony of the smell of the tea.

A number of small rooms ran off this waiting room. These were the interviewing rooms, where in reasonable privacy the clients could at last whisper out their difficulties. It seemed to me sometimes that the whole place ran on whispers, as if it were a scared place where one dared not speak in a normal voice for fear the gods might be disturbed.

I took a cup of tea to each lady in a green overall in the interviewing rooms. In every room was an old-fashioned roll-top desk with a number of baskets of files at the back of them. The baskets were marked 'Visit' or 'Letter' or 'In Hand' or 'Filing'. The clients were seated on wooden chairs at the side of the desk, and they hardly paused in their recitals to the interviewer as I brought in the tea. In one room, Dorothy Evans was riffling through the file baskets, looking for a missing file. The interview was continuing despite Dorothy's presence, and I soon learned, like her, to be quiet and unobtrusive in such a situation and never to say anything except, 'Excuse me.'

When my tray was empty, I scurried up to the kitchen on the top floor. Miss Finch was filling another cup.

'Take this down to Miss Dane – her office is next to the Cash Department.'

Miss Dane, I discovered, was the Assistant Presence. Since she was not quite so weighed down by responsibility as the Presence herself, she had time to stop her perusal of a mountain of correspondence, to ask me if I was the new office girl.

In case it was not obvious, I said, 'Yes, madam, I am.'

She was a pretty, dark-haired woman, and she smiled sweetly at me, as she said, 'I hope you will be happy here,' as if she really meant it.

'Thank you, madam,' I replied warmly, and became her devoted slave.

Tea having been served, Miss Finch and I leaned thankfully against the kitchen counters and had tea ourselves. At that time, Mary Finch was sixteen years old, a year and a half older than me, and this seemed a big gap to bridge, so our conversation was desultory.

After a few awkward minutes, we did another run up and down stairs to collect the dirty cups, and then washed them up. Our overalls still showed wet splashes from our washing up, when we again presented ourselves to Mr Ellis.

'The index cards are ready for filing,' he said. 'Get on with it.'

We obediently sorted the cards into alphabetical order and filed them. Then we took another trip to the basement waiting room to relieve Miss Lester, while she fled upstairs to the cloakroom.

Two new girls to look at caused the clients to rustle in their seats and murmur to each other behind shielding hands. There were no magazines for them to read, so their boredom must have been intense.

Miss Finch sat down at the table and I stood by her and looked around me. One wall was shelved and was packed with fat, dusty envelopes set upright.

'They're old files,' explained Miss Finch. 'If you can't find a file upstairs, it may be down here.' And as if to justify her words, the phone rang and she was requested to check if a certain file was on the shelves.

It was. And to save Miss Barker, K to Z , coming down for it, I was sent hurrying upwards with the grubby envelope. The staircases were rapidly beginning to feel like Mount Everest to me, they were so long and steep.

When I returned, a woman in a faded cotton frock and grey cardigan was standing in front of Mary. She was holding a baby and her stomach was already swollen with another child. Mary wrote down her name and address, and handed the slip to me.

'You phone it up,' she said lazily.

I took the slip as if it might bite me and reluctantly

144

went to the little cubbyhole where the phone was. Slowly, I lifted the receiver.

Immediately came the soft hello of the volunteer temporarily manning the switchboard.

I gave the name carefully, spelling it out to make sure that it was correctly recorded.

'Thank you,' said the voice from the switchboard very clearly.

I hung up the receiver on its hook and stood looking triumphantly at the phone. I had managed to use the instrument and I could hear on it. Joyfully I went back to Miss Finch. Perhaps, one day, I would be able to manage the switchboard.

Chapter twenty

After our visit to the basement waiting room, Miss Finch and I spent an hour sorting and filing index cards under Mr Ellis's eagle eye.

As her fingers flew along the drawers of cards, Miss Finch explained to me in a whisper that at half past eleven we had to go to a famous cake shop and restaurant to collect a sandwich lunch for a Committee, which would meet in the Committee Room on the top floor during the lunch hour. We had also to make coffee for the members, and lay the table.

The walk to the restaurant was not very far, but after all the stairs I had climbed in the course of the morning, it seemed a long way. Still, the fresh air blowing off the river and the bustle of the city were welcome. In this district there was little hint of the frightful effects of the Depression upon Liverpool; just an occasionally empty shop, and a larger number of offices to rent than usual. The businessmen hurrying up and down the street were well dressed, and no unemployed men hung about the street corners.

The lunch was not quite ready, so we waited unobtrusively in a corner of the cake shop and watched the fashionable crowd passing through to the restaurant at the rear. Ladies in flowered or feathered hats with veils drooping over their eyes were greeted by men in immaculate, dark suits, their neatly rolled umbrellas hooked over one arm, black felt hats held in their hands, as they ushered the ladies into the dreamland beyond. I remembered when Mother had been just such a lady meeting one of her men friends in a restaurant for lunch. She sometimes took me with her, as a sop to propriety, I presume.

My eyes wandered to the display counters. Behind the glass there was a wonderful collection of cakes, chocolate éclairs, *babas au rhum* topped with cream, *petits fours* in delicate pink, white or mauve icing, French sandwiches oozing with raspberry jam and cream and smothered in icing sugar. There was a fruit cake with at least an inch of marzipan resting on its top. It was flanked by chocolate swiss rolls, and my mouth watered. It all seemed part of a dream of long ago.

'Here, take this,' ordered Mary Finch.

She thrust a large confectioner's box into my hands and balanced another on top of it, while she turned to pay the shop assistant with money given her by the cashier.

'Be careful,' Mary warned, as we struggled through the lunch-time crowds. 'We'll get into trouble if the cakes are squashed.'

In the kitchen, we set out on plates the pretty cakes and the tiny rolls filled with different meats and wisps of mustard and cress. Then we laid the long, narrow table and made a pot of coffee, wrapping up the latter in tea towels to keep it warm.

With a last glance at the inviting table, Mary Finch hustled me out and down one floor to the silent lift.

'Committee members are allowed to use the lift,' she explained. 'You'd better know how to run it.'

I was dreadfully hungry and this announcement threw me into immediate panic. I foresaw another débâcle, like that of the switchboard.

Mary showed me how to start and stop the lift, and then said, 'Now, you try.'

Gingerly I closed the gates at the main floor, pressed the handle and, with a sense of shock, found that instead of going up we had descended to the basement waiting room. The astonished clients – they were, according to Mary, always to be referred to as clients – had seen all those preceding them sent up to the Interviewing Floor by the stairs and they were obviously surprised at this sudden arrival of a lift.

'Stupid,' hissed my teacher, who must herself have been both tired and hungry. 'Turn the handle the other way.'

I did so, and we shot upwards, passing a bewildered gentleman in a bowler hat standing on the ground floor.

We were at the top again and the lift automatically clanked to a stop. The door of the Filing Department opposite flew open. The Presence's typist, her face forbidding, asked, 'Why are you running the lift? The Secretary wishes to know.'

Trouble again. I opened my mouth like a cod fish, but it was Miss Finch who answered smartly, 'I'm teaching the new girl how to run it, ready for the Committee.'

'I see.' The typist returned to her desk.

'Phew!' exclaimed Mary. 'The old geezer's got the

ears of a cat. Now run the lift down, and stop at every floor. Try to get it level.'

We sailed straight down to the basement again, and I whispered to Mary, 'Caves, catacombs and coal mines, bargain floor.'

Mary started to giggle.

The man in the bowler hat must have decided to walk up the stairs, because the main floor, opposite the tea merchant's door, was deserted.

'Graveyards, grizzlies, golliwogs, gamps, goats, tea shop, main floor,' I announced gravely.

Mary laughed, and waited expectantly for the next floor.

'Overalls, olive oil, ostriches, offal, first floor,' I said, in the same sing-song voice of a department store lift girl.

'Secretaries, sausages, soap, Somalis, shoes, Simnel cakes.' I flung open the gate at the second floor, stepped out and bowed to Miss Finch as if she were an honoured customer and I a shop walker.

But Miss Finch looked past me, her face immobile. I whirled round. The Assistant Presence was watching me, her eyes twinkling with amusement.

Horrified, I waited for the guillotine to fall. But she was laughing, as she wagged an admonishing finger. 'The Committee will be arriving. I saw Mr Thompson walking up just now.'

'I'm sorry, Miss Dane,' said Mary, and with silent grimaces to each other we descended to the ground floor, while Miss Dane walked up to the Committee Room on the top floor which was not served by the lift.

There was a sound of running feet in the hall, and

a young man carrying a brief case almost flung himself into the lift. He was breathtakingly handsome, and his immaculate white shirt showed up a regimental tie to perfection. Before I could close the gates, he was joined by two white-haired ladies wafting a soft perfume with them. They greeted each other; and, after peeping out to see if anyone else was coming, I carefully closed the gates. The three passengers turned towards the gates and waited in silence as we travelled upwards, like a small congregation listening to a priest reciting the Creed.

At the top, I positioned the lift with a series of sharp little ups and downs, and then let the passengers out. None of them had said anything to either Miss Finch or me. The ladies loosened their furs and walked slowly up the remaining flight of stairs, while Miss Finch and I, like little marionettes, ran the lift up and down, ferrying other Committee members. Later, I learned that many of these people were members of old Liverpool families famous for their charities through several generations. They were all concerned by the sad state of their native city, and they gave generously of both time and money in an effort to help their suffering fellow citizens.

As I watched them from under lowered lids, it sometimes felt odd to me that my grandmother and grandfather had probably wined and dined with these people or their parents, had done business with them, had attended balls and concerts with them; and, there I was, so hungry that I could have eaten all the lunch waiting upstairs, running a lift for them as if I was part of the machinery.

Chapter twenty-one

I had been tired at the end of the first day of work, but by the end of the second day it seemed as if every muscle had its own particular ache. My imagination boggled at the thought of how many stairs had been climbed, how many miles walked. Even Miss Finch, who was a strong, well-fed girl, looked worn out; and I had done the same amount as she had on less food than a prisoner of war could hope for. As I trailed home, I realised that on the following day I would have to do the same work without Miss Finch's help.

At the end of the day one of the duties of the office girl, I discovered, was to collect any remaining outgoing letters from their various signatories, put them into their envelopes and take them to the nearby General Post Office and drop them in the letter box. There was always a flurry on the part of the stenographers to bring down last minute letters for signature by the Presence.

The Presence was a very hard-pressed woman and was frequently in the middle of phone calls or interviews, when the letters arrived. The stenographers laid the letters on her desk, thankfully put on their hats and coats and went home. The little office girl stood outside the office and waited for the letters to be brought out by the Presence's secretary, who was a volunteer; and on some evenings she waited and she waited.

The office clock would tick remorselessly on towards Edward's and Avril's bedtime and the hour of night school. My stomach would tighten with fear of Mother's temper if I was not there to help. And night school teachers could be very sarcastic if one was late for class.

Finally, the letters would be brought out. The pretty secretary would help me put them into their envelopes. Those to be delivered by hand were put on one side. With a smile of relief, the secretary would hand me the ones to be posted; and I would run down the stairs, across the busy streets, and dutifully drop them into the post office's mighty maw.

At home at last, I took off my hat and coat and hung them on a peg in the hall. There was no night school on that second day of work. But there was homework to do, English essays to write, arithmetic problems to solve, shorthand to practise. Then there were the beds, left from the morning, waiting to be made, dishes to wash up, Edward and Avril to wash and put to bed, clothes to be washed or sponged and pressed, all the thousand and one tasks of a large family. I sighed as I entered the living room.

The room looked different.

Everybody was present, except Fiona and Avril whom I could see through the window. They were skipping in the back yard.

The window!

It was shining clean and the grubby net curtain which usually covered it had been washed.

I glanced around. The big, old-fashioned iron grate with its side oven shone with blacking. The battered wooden chairs had been polished till all the nicks and chips in them appeared covered. The up-turned paint drums had been scoured. The mantel-piece, usually littered with bills and replies to Mother's begging letters, was dusted and tidied, the papers neatly stacked under a well-washed stone; and the alarm clock ticked merrily in the dead centre; it seemed to be sticking out its chest with pride at its pristine green paint and its twinkling glass. The worn linoleum on the floor was speckless and the piece of coconut matting in the centre had obviously received a good beating.

Mother was sitting by the fire. She had changed her work dress for a shapeless, grubby cotton frock and her bare feet were thrust into a pair of old carpet slippers. The varicose veins on her legs showed in sickening knots, and her face was lined with fatigue. She had started to darn the boys' socks ready for them to put on again in the morning, and she was frowning heavily as she pushed the big needle in and out. She looked up as I entered.

'Goodness, Mum,' I exclaimed, as I looked round admiringly. 'You have been busy. The room looks lovely.'

'Humph.' She looked down at her darning again.

I eased around the *Liverpool Echo* and gave Father a cautious peck on the cheek, in the hope that I was forgiven for going to work. And then I leaned over and gave Mother an equally careful kiss. But Mother, for once, did not seem angry with me. She said, 'Hello, dear,' rather absently and went on darning.

I picked up Edward and gave him a hug. He

laughed at me as I put him down, and then scrambled away under the table, where, judging from the dialogue, Brian and Tony had established a castle. Their imaginations were so fertile that they were able to create a whole strange world out of almost nothing, and it probably saved them in some degree from the effects of the savage reality of our life.

Mother said very mildly. 'There is some dinner in the oven for you, dear.'

Alan looked up from his book, and said, 'Hello. It's sausages.' He sounded cheerful and his red-rimmed, bright blue eyes were, as usual, friendly in their expression.

I grinned at him, and then I looked back at Mother. Sometimes I was more afraid of her when she was being kind than I was when she was not. Carefully, I moved round the back of her and opened the heavy oven door. Two sausages sat on a plate accompanied by a good tablespoonful of dried up cabbage and a whole potato. I whipped the hot plate over to the table, found a knife and fork and thankfully sat down to eat. From time to time, I took a peep at Mother's clouded face.

'The dinner's nice,' I said appreciatively. This brought no response, so I added, 'You must have worked awfully hard today, Mum.' I looked again round the room and wondered where she had got the soap, the polish and the blacking from. There had never been any money for such things while I had been keeping house. The floor must have been scrubbed with a scrubbing brush, which we did not possess, before it could be shined as it had been.

Father rose, picked the teapot off the hob and brought it to me. He looked down at me with an odd expression on his face – as if he were trying to warn me. 'Here you are, old girl,' he said kindly, as he put the pot down on the table. 'Have some tea.'

What had I said that I should not have said?

'Thanks, Daddy.'

Mother stabbed a sock to death. 'I have not been working here,' she announced icily. 'I have been in Lewis's all day, demonstrating automatic toasters.'

Alan did not look up from his book, but the eyelid furthest from Mother went down in a clear, slow wink.

'That must have been interesting,' I said firmly, as I poured a cup of well-boiled tea. 'I've never seen an automatic toaster.'

'I hope I never see another,' said Mother with feeling. Then her rage burst out of her. 'Alice – that Alice – had the temerity to walk into this house this morning, without permission, and clean this room. She actually let herself in. It's outrageous!' Mother rolled up a pair of socks and flung them into the fruit punnet we used as a sewing box.

'Alice cleaned it?' I exclaimed.

'She did and I am furious.'

'She did a marvellous job,' I said, with honest admiration.

Mother's chin quivered and her thin chest heaved, as she seized another sock and thrust her hand into it.

'I will decide when my house needs cleaning. I will not have a peasant walking in and out of here, as if she owned the place.'

I was so tired, and I thought how marvellous it would be to come home every day to a clean, tidy house, so I said pacifically, 'You know, Mummy, if she did not charge very much, it might be worth getting her to do it regularly. It would save us both.'

'She didn't charge anything,' interjected Alan. 'When she brought Edward home, she said it gave her something to do while her mother was having a nap and that Edward liked being in his own house.'

'What nonsense!' Mother said angrily.

'Where did she get the blacking from? And the polish?' I inquired, as I scraped my plate.

Alan laughed. 'She brought her own.'

Mother caught her breath and I looked quickly across at her. She was biting her lower lip and a tear ran down her face. Suddenly I understood her humiliation, and instinctively I jumped up and went over to her. I put my arm round her shaking shoulders.

'Try not to cry, Mummy,' I urged. 'Everybody knows you have been ill and she probably thought she was being kind and helpful. I know that people round here help each other a lot. They always seem to know where help is needed, because they gossip so much.'

Mother nearly choked. 'I don't want them gossiping about me,' she shouted. 'When I want help I will pay for it.'

Father had been watching the scene over his newspaper, and now he said exasperatedly, 'You should not be upset. The girl meant well. She's not going to do it again, I am sure.'

'She certainly will not,' snapped Mother. 'As you observed, I settled that point once and for all.'

I felt as if Mother had stabbed me with her darning needle. 'Don't let it be so, O Lord. Please!' I almost whispered aloud.

But it *had* happened. Alice had been dismissed as firmly as I had been the previous day. And I had yet to tell my parents about my dismissal and re-instatement.

'What about Edward?' I asked, trying to keep calm.

'Oh, you will have to stay at home. This idea of going to work is ridiculous. See what an upset it has caused to all of us. And you are worn out.'

I *was* worn out. Mother so rarely looked at me unless I had done something wrong, that I was surprised that she had noticed. But the gulf opening in front of me was so abhorrent to me that I gained a fresh surge of strength. And I fought back as if defeat would mean certain hanging in the morning.

Every member of the family joined in the battle. Mother had hysterics, Father roared, Edward howled. Avril, stretched to her full thirty inches of height, shook her finger at us all and demanded in frantic tones that we stop. Alan took my part with reckless abandon. Fiona wept and screwed her piece of skipping rope into knots as she swore she was not going to stay at home, as I suggested. From the castle under the table, the sounds of knights preparing to go out to slay a dragon ceased and two scared faces peeped out.

'Who is going to see that the boys don't get into trouble?' Mother asked dramatically, as they emerged.

'I will,' shouted Alan.

'They're big enough to look after themselves,' I screamed, most unfairly.

Brian and Tony began to bellow as they, poor innocents, suddenly became the focus of the quarrel. They must have felt that they were being abandoned by all of us.

Sometimes, in those difficult days, I identified myself with an alley cat which I had once seen engulfed in a football crowd racing down a train platform from a football special. Slipping, sliding, slithering in and out amongst the hob-nailed boots, fearing all the time that small paws would be crushed, wispy tail agonisedly trodden on; expecting any moment to feel a steel toe in the ribs flinging it over the platform edge into dark, unknown depths of misery; finding, for a second, shelter by a pile of luggage in which to lick quickly at bruised sides; only to be caught up again in the ruthless rush; looking madly for a wall up which to race or a kindly hand to sweep it up and tuck it inside a shirt, away from the terrible boots.

This time I thought that Minerva had forgotten her stepchild.

The abuse was largely verbal but the threat of physical punishment was always there. The elder children had when young all felt the weight of a cane and sound spankings with a hand; and occasionally both Father and Mother would strike out quite hard at one or the other of us. I do not think it occurred to any of us, even Alan who was growing quite tall, to strike back.

I would not yield. Mother said she would go to see the Presence and would demand my dismissal. The organisation had not, after all, purchased me, she said acidly.

Suddenly I remembered the Presence's words about a week's notice. Presumably, on my side, a week's notice would also have to be given before I could leave. I announced this triumphantly as fact.

'What rubbish,' shrieked Mother. She was thrashing round the small room like a tiger, and the children moved mechanically to get out of her way as she advanced on each one of them.

Father, who was still sitting in his chair, as if it offered a modicum of safety, the newspaper crumpled in his clenched fists, said in a more normal voice, 'She is correct. Either we pay a week's salary to them or she must work the week.'

Fiona wailed loudly, 'I don't want to stay at home.'

'You'll have to,' I said mercilessly. 'Fi, you'll have to. I have done my bit. You must take a turn. It's only till Edward is big enough to go to school.'

'I won't,' she screamed. She flung her skipping rope to the floor. 'No.'

'No,' Mother flashed at me. 'Oh, no. You are not going to push your responsibilities on to poor Fiona. She is much too frail, poor darling.'

Chapter twenty-two

The need to give notice saved me.

Fiona was ordered to stay at home with Edward for the following two days. Mother's contract with the toaster manufacturer expired on Thursday night; she would start a new contract at another store the following Tuesday. This, I argued, would give her time to arrange some fresh care for Edward.

Poor little Edward. Poor Fiona, red-faced and deeply resentful. Mother actually smiled, however, when I presented her with my total earning for the week, less fourpence for contributions to National Health and Unemployment Insurance and another penny contributed to a hospital fund. She hardly heard me when I explained that the following week, I would be earning only an office girl's pay.

In the office, I ran so hard and whispered so softly that my appointment was confirmed, despite my gauche manners and poor grooming.

A few weeks later, the other girls asked me to accompany them to the cinema. Bashfully, I refused, owning up that I did not have the money. They looked at me askance and did not ask me again for a number of years; perhaps they thought I did not like them.

Night school came to an end and I passed the examinations. This gave me more time to help Mother at home. The office staff, in turn, went away for two weeks' holiday to the mountains or the sea-side. They usually went with their parents and came back with breathtaking stories of the boys they had met. They giggled behind the stacks of files until Mr Ellis roared at them to return to their work. He seemed to be the only person who spoke above a thin whisper.

I had no adventures to share with the girls. I was not entitled to a holiday that year, and my world of screaming family rows, of creditors, of pawnbrokers, of the lack of the most basic human needs, seemed to be so divorced from the experience of the staff, that there was no common ground. I was obsessed with the need to survive, with simple worries, like how to squeeze a pair of rayon stockings out of Mother, or even darning silk with which to mend the ones I wore. I was totally dependent upon the whims of Mother. She seemed to take it for granted that anything I earned was hers, and this idea stayed with her throughout my working life. Girls did not need money for expenses; boys did.

One day, the Presence told me sharply to tidy up my hair. It was pay day and, in despair, I took out of my nine shillings and sevenpence a single bright shilling. A comb cost twopence, some hairclips a penny. Ninepence would buy a good, stout pair of rayon stockings.

Mother was so infuriated that she tried to snatch Joan's old handbag off me in order to extract the shilling, but I whisked it under me and sat on it and, tearfully, refused to move.

Father came home and walked into the middle of

the scene, and I appealed to him, because sometimes he did seem to regard me as a human being, even if I was a girl. Without any hesitation, he said I should keep the shilling, and have one each week, so I thankfully fled with my handbag to the kitchen and left my parents to fight it out.

The weekly shilling was usually spent on second-hand articles of clothing. But I soon learned not to leave any pieces of clothing at home unless they were wet from washing, because they would be immediately pawned; stockings or gloves would be used by Mother herself or given to Fiona. On days when there was nothing to take for my lunch, I would buy a penny bread roll from Lunt's bakery near the office.

An overwhelming ambition in those days was to be able to afford from Lunt's a roll packed with cheese. These cost twopence, however, and I had to content myself with buying them for other members of the staff or just looking longingly at them through the bakery's steamy window.

And so I struggled blindly on from day to day. The trees in Princes Park, where on Saturday afternoons I took Edward to play, turned yellow and carpeted a neat circle of grass beneath them with curled-up leaves. Wet days became more frequent, and I delivered the letters each morning in shoes that became quickly sodden; the cardboard put into them to block up the holes disintegrated, and tender bare soles were exposed to the pavement. I caught so many colds that the days when I was without one became ones of rejoicing. Liverpool air is always damp and, in those days, was filled with black particles from a myriad of chimneys, so that nasal catarrh and bronchitis were endemic and gave rise to the famous, snuffly Liverpool accent. Like many of the population I blew my nose through my fingers on to the pavement, and kept my single handkerchief for neat dabs at my nose in the office.

Alan reached the age of fourteen in November and left school shortly afterwards. I was plunged into bitter and unfair jealousy, as I watched him set out for his first job as office boy in a new suit bought for the occasion from Marks & Spencers. In his pocket he carried a bit of lunch wrapped in an old margarine paper and a penny for the tram, so that he would not have to climb the long hill home. He was given pocket money as a matter of course, so my battle evidently helped him. He was intelligent and quick-witted and very articulate. He had snatched the job from dozens of other applicants and deserved all the help my parents could give him.

The life of an office boy was very hard. In a tall, gloomy, Victorian building, he worked from eight-thirty in the morning until six o'clock at night and until one o'clock on Saturdays, for a wage of seven shillings and sixpence a week. Office boys were commonly hit when they made mistakes or if they dared to answer their seniors back, and the tight-lipped bookkeeper who taught him how to keep accounts was very heavy handed. He was still far from being fully developed and, like me, was painfully thin. Since he spoke 'with an olly in his mouth', he had been in many fights at school – it is not only sparrows who attempt to destroy those different from themselves – and sometimes, in the absence of the bookkeeper at lunch, a general fight would break out amongst the young men in the office. Though he fought back fairly skilfully, I can remember seeing bruises across his buttocks where he had been beaten with an old-fashioned rounded ruler.

Attached to the church was a troop of Boy Scouts and Alan had joined this. Although we were certainly not the poorest family in the parish, the Scoutmaster must have found it impossible to obtain money from my parents for a uniform for him, and, therefore, provided him with one. He once went away to camp with them and returned looking strong and rosy and very freckled, but the fair skin soon became white again and the beguiling freckles faded, to be replaced by acne in its worst forms. Great boils covered his face and neck. A cheerful expression helped to compensate for this affliction. His tousled cowlick was neatly slicked back with the aid of brilliantine and the black pocket comb tucked into his jacket pocket. His pale skin gained a slight ruddiness as, like me, he ran through the streets of Liverpool, in and out of horse and motor traffic, delivering letters and messages.

Like me, Alan suffered from the lack of a raincoat and from inadequate footwear. Liverpool shares with Ireland not only Irish inhabitants but Irish weather. When it is not actually raining, there is still a misty dampness which seems to penetrate one's bones. Older people always seem to be complaining about 'me rheumatism' or 'me arthritics' and say that they 'hurt something wicked' on wet days.

Alan, Brian and Tony all played cricket in the street, often with a beer bottle as a wicket and a piece of board as a bat. Alan had had the advantage, when quite a small boy, of playing the game in better circumstances. A couple of professionals had taken an amused interest in the little eager beaver who haunted their practice ground and had coached him. This acquired ability had led him into the school team. One of his older colleagues at work gave him his old cricket bat and pads, and this enhanced his chances of playing with other teams after he left school. He got a lot of pleasure from these games.

He also went to night school. He always says he learned a lot there. But he did not stay in the system very long, and he probably learned much more in the Auxiliary Air Force, which he joined a few years later.

I rejoiced in his good beginning in the business world. Because my parents kept pressing me to stay at home again and be the unpaid housekeeper, I was most unchristianly envious of the interest and encouragement lavished on him by both Mother and Father. I cried for hours through freezing winter nights, and prayed frequently and earnestly for strength to keep my temper. I was convinced that most of my misery was caused by lack of self-control over envy and bad temper. It was a long time before I realised that there is a limit to anybody's self-control; and that the only sin I had committed was to be born to my Mother at a time when she would otherwise have divorced my Father. She could never forgive me for it.

Chapter twenty-three

As autumn merged into winter the children began to look forward to Christmas, having been reminded of its coming by Brian and Tony's extra choir practices. For years, Fiona and I secreted all kinds of bits of wool, old socks and cotton scraps, and out of them we manufactured gifts for the family. Golliwogs and rabbits emerged from the socks, hand-hemmed handkerchiefs, handkerchief cases, pin cushions and hair tidies, prettily covered boxes and pyjama cases were made from the cotton scraps. I once made Fiona a doll's bed out of a shoebox; it was complete with little blankets and a bedspread, and she joyfully put her tattered doll into it. The doll was her only treasure from our old home. It was dreadfully dirty, and its papier mâché feet and hands were nearly worn out; but its glass eyes still opened and closed and it still had some hair.

Another time, I made a horse and cart for Edward. The horse was made out of corks found in the street. It had wobbly legs made out of slivers of firewood. The cart, which was a carton from a box of matches, had high wheels made from the tiny lids of ointment tins, also found in the street gutters. Though it was not a very robust toy he played with it for several days before it fell to bits.

From their choir money, Brian and Tony bought

little gifts for everybody. One of my most treasured possessions is a pottery black cat given me by Tony and, until recently, I had a tiny pottery donkey with a red pincushion on its back, bought for me by Brian. When, after forty-five years, I recently smashed the donkey I stood over the scattered bits and cried. Both these treasures travelled half way round the world with me. Another treasure is a crocheted red and yellow egg cosy made for me by Avril in one of her earliest sewing classes. Sometimes I take it out and think of the small, determined little girl stabbing away with a crochet hook too big for her fingers.

Alan's shilling a week was strictly for pocket money, so he bought us all kinds of delightful gifts, like bottles of perfume and talcum powder from Woolworth's.

My parents always tried to make Christmas pleasant for the younger children. Only the first two Christmases in Liverpool were without any real effort at celebration, and for both of those we enjoyed one of the Christmas boxes of food distributed to the poor of Liverpool during the festive season.

For two Christmases after I began work, a mysterious stranger telegraphed us five pounds. We never discovered who sent it but it provided a dinner and a stocking full of small gifts for the little ones.

Alan and I, like all working people, had two days' holiday. Such was his exhaustion that on any holiday Alan slept until midday. For Fiona and me, however, there was never such a luxury. Boys needed rest; girls could manage without. Brian and Tony had to be got up and given their breakfast in time for them to sing at the Christmas services. Edward, like most little boys, was awake at sun-up, as was Father. On Sundays and holidays, Mother stayed late in bed and Avril slept late, too. Holidays for me were not a time for relaxation, and I was always thankful to escape back to work. At work, people occasionally said, 'Thank you.'

In February, the cold and the lack of food caught up with me, and I fell ill. I staggered round the spinning office, dumbly terrified that if I said I was ill I would be dimissed, as girls in shops sometimes were. There was the further fear that if I had to stay at home, Mother would find means of keeping me there. She looked after Edward on days when she had no work; occasionally Fiona would be kept at home to mind him, and on other days he was handed round to various neighbouring women to be watched for a few hours. The problem was solved when he reached the age of four and could run along to school with Avril. Nothing seemed to disturb him much. He was used to a large family and seemed to add any strangers to that family. He was obedient and had a tranquillity which the rest of us lacked. Perhaps he realised that, despite the fights which raged over his head, he was never attacked and we all loved him very much.

Though the gulf between Mother and me had, since infancy, appeared to me to be unbridgeable, she had recently begun to talk idly to me as if I were a woman. Only the surface of her mind seemed to be engaged in the conversation; somewhere deep underneath lay the real woman, with true passions and motives. But it was better than nothing. Despite this small break, I still dreaded that she would again pass over her family responsibilities to me. So that in overwhelming fear I fumbled about the office making tea, sorting index cards, going out to deliver letters, while Mr Ellis ranted that I was more than usually slow and stupid. My chest hurt and my throat hurt and I ached all over as I sought to please him. On the second day, like an Edwardian heroine, I collapsed quietly into a chair.

Everybody was concerned and kind. Smelling salts were thrust under my nose, tea was made; and, when I could get up, Mary was instructed to escort me to the tram. I was not very clear about what was happening and was shivering, as Mary bundled me into the vehicle.

I sat down by a workman in torn work clothes, and took out my last penny from Joan's handbag. I dropped it, and it rattled away down towards the front of the vehicle. The workman looked up from his *Echo*, while I sat aghast, feeling that even if I could find the coin under the feet of all the other passengers, I would collapse if I bent over to retrieve it.

The middle-aged workman next to me was staring, as the skinny conductor, rattling his money bag as warning, came down the aisle to collect the fares. I sat silent, waiting to be thrown off at the next stop because I did not have the fare.

The man folded up his paper and proffered a sixpence to the conductor. 'Two woons, lad,' he said.

The conductor punched two tickets, handed them to him, and wandered on down the aisle. The man handed one of the tickets to me. ' 'ere ya, luv,' he said, his rough red face beaming.

My voice seemed to come from far away, as I said, 'Thank you. Thank you very much. You are most kind.'

'Aye, that's all right, luv.'

He looked down at his folded paper and I looked down at the stubby fingers holding it; they were scarred from many cuts about the knuckles and the nails were broken to the quick. The memory of them and of their wonderfully perceptive owner stayed with me through the illness that followed.

Contributions to National Health Insurance entitled workers to the services of a doctor. When my parents came home and found me shivering in my bed, they sent for the general practitioner with whom I had registered my name.

He came marching into the smelly, bug-ridden bedroom, went straight to the window and flung it open, waited for a moment and then closed it partially. In the light of a candle held by Mother, he examined me and diagnosed influenza and tonsillitis. The tonsillitis had caused an ear infection. He ordered that more covering than the single blanket and old overcoat on my bed be put over me, a fire be made in the bedroom, the window kept slightly open. He painted my throat with tannic acid, put drops in my ears and ordered aspirin to alleviate the influenza. He was a handsome man with a very white skin and a large black moustache. He was exceedingly kind to me over the three weeks of my illness, coming in daily to paint my throat, and assumed an almost Godlike character in my romantic mind.

He also ordered a light diet of milk, eggs and orange juice. This seemed to be out of the question. But Mother did make bread and milk for me, and for the rest I had Oxo cubes dissolved in hot water, toast and tea. When there was enough coal, a fire was made for me by Father, but most of the time we were too short of fuel, despite the fact that my kind employer continued to send my wages by mail and Mother cashed the postal orders.

For days I lay in my cold bed watching the sleet and rain of February through the dusty, finger-marked window, too exhausted by fever and pain to think. The children were used to my retiring temporarily to bed with bouts of tonsillitis and rarely came to see me except at bedtime. Edward had been moved from my bed in case of infection and shared my parents' bed; but as soon as the fever had departed Mother used me as a baby-sitter for him, which meant I dared not sleep during the day.

Once I could walk about the house, I asked the doctor to certify me as fit. I told him that if I was away much longer, I might lose my job. This was such a common reason for going back to work before one was fit, that he signed the certificate. I washed and ironed my blouse and panties, mended my stockings and the next day reported to work.

It seemed as if the staircases had grown longer in my absence and the distances I had to walk to deliver letters seemed to have expanded to infinity. Several times I had to lean against a wall until bouts of faintness passed.

It took such a very long time to walk home that

Father became anxious and set out to meet me. We came face to face beside the Philharmonic Hall, where he had paused to glance at the tattered black and white posters announcing their concerts.

His cheap navy blue suit shone at the elbows and seat, and it hung on him. He looked cold and forlorn without a raincoat, and his thin, lined face showed anxiety, as he hastened towards me.

'Where have you been?' he inquired, as he took my elbow and turned towards home. 'We have been worried about you.'

'I had to wait for the letters to be signed before I posted them,' I muttered, my breath coming in short gasps after the effort of climbing the hill.

'You should have taken the tram home,' Father said. 'You're not fit to walk.'

'I didn't have any money,' I wailed suddenly, all the misery of years bursting from me in one long, subdued howl.

'Good God! I thought it was arranged that you should have a shilling a week for pocket money and fares.' He stopped and looked into my woebegone face.

'Mother didn't have any of my wages left, when I asked her this morning,' I sobbed.

He clicked his tongue in annoyance. 'Dear Lord!' he exclaimed in exasperation.

This was the first time for many years that Father and I had been together without any other member of the family present, and it was as if he came out of his usual absent state and really looked at me. The sight seemed to have some impact.

I continued to wail softly as we inched our way along dark Myrtle Street and turned into Catherine Street, while he supported me by the elbow.

My sobs receded and I turned towards him. His large, high-bridged nose was scarlet from acne roseola, the rest of the skin an unhealthy yellow. His shirt and collar had reached an off-white colour from too much washing with too little soap, and his trousers badly needed pressing. His expression was so sad that I nearly burst into tears again. When he was not absorbed in a book or quarrelling with Mother, he could be quite light-hearted and very witty, but now I was again reminded of a butterfly caught in a rainstorm. With horrid clarity, I saw, not a vague, exasperating figure called Father, but a defeated man; and for a moment I walked with him through the morass of despair into which he had fallen. There seemed nothing left of the cheerful young man, described to me by Grandma, who had gone off to war, despite his short-sightedness, and ended up in the forests of Russia. My first memories of him had been of a voice screaming with terror in the night. He suffered scarifying nightmares of his war experiences while he tried to re-establish himself in a post war world, which was fed up with returning soldiers and their needs. He was a cultivated man, clever in his way, but now he worked as a clerk for the city, earning more than he handed over to Mother, but still very little. With the rest of the family, he suffered very much from the lack of intellectual companionship as well as lack of food and comfort.

As we slowly made our way along Catherine Street,

we began to feel comfortable together, like walking wounded helping each other along. Though we did not talk much, because I was too exhausted, a feeling of understanding began to grow between us.

Before we entered the house, Father took a sixpence from his waistcoat pocket and pressed it into my hand.

'Come home on the tram every day,' he ordered.

I stared down at the tiny silver coin, too tired even to thank him, and then nodded agreement and slipped the coin into my handbag.

He pulled the string hanging from the letterbox and released the latch of the front door. He swung the door open and stepped back on to the pavement with a little bow, to allow me to pass in first. Poignantly, that polite gesture brought home to me, more than anything else, how different he was from the men who lived round us. Little Avril once expressed a similar idea. She said, 'I love Daddy. He is so gentle and he is the only man in the street who wears a collar.'

Chapter twenty-four

I soon gained strength again and, through long days, slid silently between the patient, smelly clients, carrying cups of tea or files or messages. Sometimes I felt like advising the quietly courteous interviewers that our funds would do as much good if they were simply scattered in the back streets and left for the inhabitants to pick up. In large areas of Liverpool there was barely an inhabitant who was not in distress. Workless, half-starved, they were packed into deteriorating houses lacking proper toilets or running water. They were often shiftless and stupid, many spent their money on drink and some on drugs, but their need was blatantly manifest to anyone who cared to walk down the long treeless streets and through the narrow courts. Born and bred in such shocking conditions, who could blame them for seeking at every opportunity the garish warmth of the public houses on almost every corner?

It was pathetic to watch the clients doing their best not to use coarse language before the gently-bred ladies of our organisation. Their usually loud voices were lowered to the whispers of the confessional, as they hesitantly chose words that would please, not offend. They never laughed.

In fact, nobody laughed, except the shorthand typists in their isolated nest on the top floor. It was not an environment calculated to raise the spirits of a sad and sick fifteen-year old.

Grandma had, however, taught me to read out of the Bible, and I believed firmly in miracles. I had also not yet totally lost my belief in fairies, particularly Robin Goodfellow, a wicked sprite who sometimes snatched cups from my careless fingers and smashed them on the floor or who lost my pencils and dropped the hairpins out of my hair.

When the Presence sent for me one sunny May morning, therefore, I was expecting to be upbraided for the breakage of a cup and saucer, Robin Good-fellow having been rather busy the previous day. Instead, she performed a miracle.

I stood humbly before her desk, blue overall crumpled and splashed, greasy hair untidily knotted into a bun at the nape of my neck. Fortunately, she was too busy to look up at me.

She had a letter in her hand and she announced, as she read it, that I was entitled to two weeks' holiday that summer and had been granted a free holiday in a place called Kent's Bank. Mr Ellis would tell me when I could go, and a train ticket would be sent to me by the charity concerned. It did not strike me at the time that she might have asked me if I would like to go. I was ordered to depart for Kent's Bank on a date to be arranged.

Beside myself with excitement, I thanked her and fled back upstairs to the kitchen, where I stood quivering in front of the sink. A holiday! An un-dreamed of luxury. A miracle.

Later, I cautiously inquired of one of the filing

clerks if she knew where Kent's Bank was. She looked derisively at me for a moment and then sniggered. That little choking laugh told me that a recipient of charity was contemptible, and that she knew why I asked.

'It's on Morecambe Bay,' she said, and turned superciliously back to her file sorting.

Terribly hurt, I slunk back to the kitchen.

*

As I ate potatoes and cabbage and gravy, saved for me from the hot meal Mother had made at tea time, I told her about the holiday.

'It's all free, Mummy. Even the train ticket. Except I think I would simply have to have a night-gown and some walking shoes – if you could get them, Mummy.'

'I can't afford them,' said Mother simply. She was sitting in the easy chair, Edward on her lap, and smoking a cigarette.

'It is time you provided things like that for yourself, now that you are at work.' She took a slow pull at the cigarette and exhaled the smoke through her nostrils. 'You must have had a rise in salary since you started. You have been working for over a year now.'

Startled, I blinked at her. I had hardly given a thought to pay increases. I had concentrated solely on retaining my job.

'No, Mummy. I've never had a rise – only a reduction the first week. I'm still the office girl.'

Mother's eyebrows rose. 'That's absurd. You must have had an increase.'

'Honestly, Mummy. I haven't. I would have told you if I had.'

Her lips twisted and she stared hostilely at me. It was clear that she did not believe me.

My throat constricted. Then I said stiffly, 'I don't cheat, Mummy.'

'They don't have money to give increases,' interjected Father, looking up from his book, laid on the table in front of him beside a half-drunk cup of tea. 'Helen should go. She still doesn't look well. Perhaps we could get a one pound cheque to buy the things she needs. Try. See what you can do.'

While they argued and Mother fretted about the peremptoriness of the Presence, who had obviously not considered that my help might be needed at home, I rescued Avril from a fight on the front pavement and put her and Edward to bed. Avril always wanted to be included in the boys' games; and this time they had not allowed her to join in a game of marbles and she was in a howling tantrum over it. She transferred some of her furious frustration to me, as I hauled her into bed and told her in true sisterly fashion to shut up.

It was a further miracle which found me standing on the doorstep of a fine stone mansion in Kent's Bank run as a guest house by an organisation which used its profits to provide free holidays for the less fortunate. The June sun warmed my back and the clear, sharp smell of the sea wafted round me. In my hand I held a brown paper bag containing a clean blouse and panties, a nightgown and a toothbrush. On my feet I wore a second-hand pair of boy's shoes.

Fiona had volunteered the loan of her raincoat which was a little short on me, but made me look quite neat. All the children had been delighted that I was to go on a holiday, though it was clear from their wistful faces that they wished they could come, too.

In answer to my timorous knock, a middle-aged man, swarthy and black-haired, ushered me in and up a fine, well-carpeted staircase, to a large bedroom containing six single beds.

'You are the first arrival, so choose whichever bed you like,' he said with a cheerful grin. 'You can put your toilet things on the dressing-table there and clothes in the wardrobe.' He gestured towards two enormous pieces of shining Edwardian furniture.

'I'd enjoy being by the window,' I replied shyly, pointing to the furthest bed which stood close to a tall light window draped in white net curtains. Through the window I could see pine trees waving in the breeze and a dazzling glimpse of the sea.

'Fine,' he said. 'Come downstairs to the lounge and have some tea, as soon as you are ready.'

I smiled my thanks and he went away.

Feeling very nervous, I put the paper bag in the wardrobe, and then like a cat in a new place I walked round the room, examining the peerless white pillows on the beds, looking down at the highly polished linoleum on the floor, and finally stopping to wash my hands in a tiny basin in a corner. I combed my hair and redid my bun in front of the spotted dressing table mirror, and then cautiously opened the bedroom door and ventured downstairs.

The lounge was full of chattering men and women,

who all seemed much older than me, and I hesitated in the doorway while the scene came into clearer focus.

An elderly gentleman was sitting on a settee directly opposite the doorway. When he looked up from his teacup and saw me, he smiled, and evidently realised that I was feeling very shy. He motioned me to come over and sit by him, which I did, perching nervously on the edge of the settee.

He had a large, grey moustache and heavy black eyebrows under which bright blue eyes twinkled merrily. He took a pipe out of his mouth and said, 'Just arrived?' I nodded, and he put down his teacup. 'I'll get you some tea. Do you take milk and sugar?'

I assented with another shy nod, and he went to the tea table and returned with tea and three biscuits. He pulled a small table forward and set the cup in front of me.

'There we are,' he announced. His voice was deep, with a pleasant Welsh sing-song to it. He sat down beside me and took up his own cup again. He had put his pipe away in the pocket of his finely cut tweed jacket.

'My name is Emrys Hughes,' he said. 'And that's my brother, Gwyn, over there.' He gestured towards the mantelpiece against which leaned a tall, thin man, also grey-haired, talking to a lady in a green dress. 'What's your name?'

I told him, and, while I sipped my tea, he asked where I came from and whether I was still at school. Each question came out in such a breezy, cheerful manner that I was soon relaxed and laughing with him. He told me that he and his brother owned two big drapery shops in North Wales, that he himself had had a heart attack at the beginning of the year, so he had come to Kent's Bank for a holiday. He had prevailed upon his bachelor brother to come with him, and they had left the businesses to the tender mercies of managers.

The teacups were removed, and still we gossiped. For the first time for many years, I was among people who knew nothing about me and judged me by what they saw. Gwyn brought the lady in green over to us. She proved to be a school teacher, who had already been at Kent's Bank for a week. Emrys looked at a heavy gold pocket watch which he took out of his top pocket, suggested that we all go for a stroll in the grounds and then eat dinner at the same table. So, much to the amusement of the older people, I spent a happy half hour running about among the trees, trying to get close to one of the many squirrels, and arrived at the dinner table glowing with the fresh air and the happy anticipation of an adequate meal.

The staff who served the meal seemed to be accustomed to very hungry people, and I ate my way through three plates of meat and vegetables and two of pudding. Emrys, who had to keep his weight down, he said, leaned back in his chair and watched me speculatively, while Gwyn and Margaret, the school teacher, chipped me about how such a small person could find room for so much food.

Having lived so much with Grandma, I felt quite at home with older people. I lost my nervousness completely, my usual gauche manners gave way to the good conduct instilled in me as a child, and I felt so happy I thought I would explode. Emrys had a way of sitting quietly and giving complete and careful attention to what was said to him. He would run his tobacco-stained fingers through his thick, grey hair, worn rather longer than was then the fashion, and smile, and comment or argue carefully on any subject discussed with me, as if I was an adult whose ideas were important to him. I was unused to anyone giving me their full attention and if I had been less innocent, I might have been troubled at such affability. But as I responded to his good-humoured teasing I knew only a great gaiety and lightness of heart. A liveliness I did not know I had began to emerge.

The first two days of the holiday were taken up with long, organised walks in the countryside, broken in the middle by a picnic lunch. The guests were divided into two groups, those who could take very long walks and those who preferred easier ones. Since both Emrys and I had been ill, we chose the easier walks and Gwyn and his school teacher came along with us.

I now shared the bedroom with five mill girls from Rochdale. All of them had been ill and said frankly that they, too, were enjoying free holidays. They all had several changes of clothing and enough money to buy tickets for the bus trips, later in the week, and to purchase endless sweets and ice cream cones from the village shop. They ignored me, and kept up a raucous conversation amongst themselves. Though I had often heard foul language in the streets of Liverpool,

I had never lived with people who used it, and I was frequently shocked and sickened by them. They also came on the easy walks, but fortunately stayed within their own group.

I danced along beside Emrys, through forest glades dappled with sunshine or along the sides of fields waving silvery green with growing oats. Occasionally, Gwyn would make us stop, while Emrys sat down to rest. He carried a piece of macintosh in his pocket and when a convenient wall or bench did not present itself, he spread the macintosh on the ground and sat on that. While he regained his breath, I would cast around, picking wild flowers or small sprays of fresh green foliage, which one of the staff would put in a vase on the dining table for me. Emrys did not know the names of many of the plants, but I had learned their names from Edith and was able to identify them for him.

Though I had handed to Mother three weeks' salary paid in advance, she had not seen fit to give me any money. I had only a few pennies in my purse, because I had spent most of the three weekly shillings on stockings. This made it impossible for me to buy tickets for the coach tour arranged for the third day.

Emrys and Gwyn had not yet come down to breakfast, so I ate the meal rather soberly in the company of Margaret and another middle-aged lady. Margaret was herself convalescing after a dose of influenza and we compared our respective illnesses and then talked about books.

'See you later,' she said gaily, and I nodded. I went

up to the empty bedroom and wondered how to employ the day. I heard the arrival of the motor coach and the bustle of departure, as I sat with a copy of Lytton's *Last Days of Pompeii* in my lap. I had already read the story twice and this seemed to hold true of all the books in the lounge downstairs. Finally, I tossed it aside. I would have a bath. I had tried several times since my arrival to do this, but the bathroom had invariably been occupied. Today, however, all the other guests had gone out so I could take my time about it.

The bath was a huge, Victorian tub, left over from the time when the house had been a private home. I turned on its great brass taps and let the water thunder in until it was quite deep. There was a large, used tablet of soap in a wire basket stretched across the bath. Quickly I stripped off and stepped in.

This was the first bath I had had for four years and the water rippling across my stomach felt odd. I looked down at long, slender legs wavering beneath the water, at a stomach which stuck out too much like that of a hungry child, at surprisingly prominent young breasts, at arms so thin they looked like sticks. The skin was a dull yellow, almost bronze in places. I had not looked at myself properly since I was a child, in that long ago world which we had left so precipitously. As I soaked in the hot water, I remembered how Father had told his biggest creditor to sell up his house and its contents, and how he had walked out of it, allowing us to take nothing with us, except the clothing we were wearing and a blanket to cover his sick wife and newest child. He knew nothing of his rights to clothes and bedding, to the minima of existence. With this one quixotic gesture, he had deprived the family of all that even the most hopeless debtor was legally entitled to. His last money had been spent on train tickets to Liverpool, his home city, which did not want him.

I kneeled up in the water, dipped my head in and then soaped it thoroughly. Three times the brown locks were soaped and rinsed. Then the thin body was soaped until it looked like a snowman. The water was covered with grey soap suds.

Like a dripping muskrat, I climbed out, emptied the bath and began to refill it.

The door burst open and a young, male member of the staff rushed in, pulling off his apron as he came. He was well into the huge bathroom, before he realised that I was standing there naked, one hand on the brass tap.

He stopped, his startled face registering shock. Then he blushed hotly.

'I say, I am sorry!' he exclaimed, and turned and fled.

I was so used to being intruded upon by my brothers in a house where all washing had to be done in the kitchen that I was undisturbed. But I did for a moment wonder why he should be so flabbergasted. A girl in her skin was nothing special as far as I could see.

I repeated the scrubbing and, when I finally emerged from the bathroom, hair wrapped in a towel like a turban, I was scarlet from head to heel.

I drew back the net curtains and sat down by the

window to dry my hair in the breeze. Such quietness enfolded me as I had not known before. Leisurely I combed the wet hair over my shoulders, and watched the sun glancing on the sea. I could smell the salt and, closer to hand, the pine trees in the garden. For the first time for years I had nothing to do. It was as if every nerve slowly loosened and relaxed. Three nights of deep, warm sleep and two days of stacks of food had helped to heal both mind and body.

I sat on the hard bedroom chair for a long time, the two rows of carelessly made beds behind me, the fine view framed by the window in front of me. My mind was empty. There was no past, no nagging family, nothing. No future, except the happy anticipation of welcoming Emrys Hughes and the other kindly guests when they returned, and then eating and eating and eating.

A train arriving at the nearby station roused me. I got up and went to the spotty mirror to arrange my hair in a bun again.

I peered short-sightedly at the image in the mirror and was surprised at what I saw. The hair, usually so straight because of its greasy coating, now waved softly down each side of the thin cheeks; its mousy brown carrying in it a rich red burnish. Surprised, I coaxed it into deeper waves.

From under smooth black brows, large green eyes, no longer bloodshot, stared sadly back at me. A few lumpy spots marred a complexion which was surprisingly white. I smiled cautiously at myself. The teeth were not straight and were tinged with yellow. I had scrubbed them well but I had no toothpaste.

With newly awakened vanity, I decided I had a nice smile. I wondered if make-up would cover the spots, and then sighed because there was no money for such luxuries. Telling myself to stop playing Narcissus, I put my hair up, taking care, however, not to draw it back too tightly and spoil the waves.

Lunch was not served in the holiday home to guests, so I went without. It was probably as well, as it gave an over-taxed digestive system time to recuperate. I spent the rest of the day washing my spare blouse and panties and ironing them dry with an iron borrowed from the kitchen. Then I went for a long walk.

The lanes had all the bright greenery of June, but last year's leaves lay sodden at the bottom of puddles formed by overnight rain. They reminded me of winter.

I dreaded the winter. Another year of cold, sopping wet feet, of piercing wind, of long stone staircases to be climbed, of shivering in a freezing bed. Another winter, too, of incredible loneliness.

Fiona is growing up, I comforted myself. She will be company. Yet instinct told me that Fiona would never really communicate with me; she was too crushed, too determined never to be caught out of character, as a passive, pliable, inoffensive, obliging person, guaranteed not to answer back. The steel which I felt lay deep within her would be used for her own self-defence. She would crouch behind it, hiding any real feeling lest someone take offence. Just as I had been cast as a maiden aunt, she had been cast by my parents as a lovely girl who would make a good marriage which would help to raise the family again to its former stature. And yet, sometimes, I thought that Fiona might surprise my parents more than I ever could. As with the rest of the children, I could give Fiona love, but she was incapable of giving me friendship.

After my walk I tidied my windblown hair and then went down to the lounge. There was a number of women's magazines in a magazine rack and I curled up on a settee with these in excited anticipation.

Except for *Peg's Paper* which Edith had allowed me to read when I was small, I had not seen any women's magazines, and I soon was engrossed in enthralling stories in which the heroine was always blonde and invariably won the hero over the machinations of a dark sultry villainess. The kisses were passionate.

Chapter twenty-five

The bus disgorging a noisy crowd of returning guests put an end to my quiet day. I reluctantly uncurled myself from the settee and put down the magazine I had been reading. Emrys came puffing into the lounge, grey raincoat flying behind him, pipe aglow like a watchman's stove. He was followed more slowly by his brother, Gwyn.

'Why didn't you come?' he asked. 'We missed you, didn't we Gwyn?'

Gwyn smiled kindly down at me. 'Yes, we did,' he assured me.

I went pink with embarrassment, and said, 'I thought I'd have a quiet day. Did you enjoy the trip?'

'I'd have enjoyed it a lot more if you had been there,' Emrys replied roundly, and playfully pinched my cheek.

Now I was blushing at the compliment. He evidently saw it, as he struggled out of his coat, and laughed.

'Well, I've made sure you come on the other trips. Gwyn and I have bought tickets for all of 'em for you. Now you *have* to come.' He gusted with laughter, and Gwyn chuckled and said, 'Well, we hope you will.'

'That's immensely kind of you both,' I told them, laughing myself, because I could not help it.

While Gwyn helped Margaret off with her coat,

Emrys stood in front of me, sturdy legs apart, while he struck matches to relight his pipe. He had told me that he was not supposed to smoke, but he could not give it up. As he gossiped about the lakes they had seen, I wondered what he would think if he saw my poverty-stricken home. Both brothers were obviously prosperous; both had gone to the prayer meeting held in the lounge each evening and both had joined earnestly in the prayers that were offered; kindness and thoughtfulness in small things was obvious in every move they made. They were very different from anybody I had ever met before. I could well imagine them behind their drapery shop counters, cheerfully and patiently dispensing everything from two pennyworth of buttons to forty yards of damask for curtains.

As the fortnight progressed, my friendship with Emrys deepened. I began to feel a real affection for the man, but such was my innocence that I never considered what he might be feeling. He was so much older than me.

Once, when he held my hand during a bus trip, some of the ladies saw it. They teased me and said I had made a conquest. This embarrassed me, because I felt that anybody could see I was incapable of conquering any man; I was too plain.

He never overstepped the bounds of propriety, however, and I never felt frightened with him. A couple of days before the holiday was due to end, he wrote out his home address for me, and said he hoped I would come to see him.

'My wife died three years ago,' he said simply.

'Gwyn and I keep house together in a flat over one of the shops. But my sister lives nearby, and you could stay with her.'

I doubted in my mind that I would ever manage to travel as far as North Wales, but the idea gave me much pleasure, and I said with genuine enthusiasm, 'I would love that.'

He looked at me very soberly for a moment, and then said, 'Would you?'

I nodded.

He grinned at me. 'Then we'll arrange it.'

On the last day of the holiday, we all went to see Cartmel Priory, and were ambling round the old church, behind our guide, when Emrys stopped suddenly and began to gasp for breath. He clutched his chest and turned and stumbled into a pew to sit down. The rest of the party had moved on ahead a little.

I leaned over the side of the pew and put my arm round his shoulder. 'What is it, Emrys?' But I knew what it was. I had seen it happen to Father when he was a young man. 'I'll get Gwyn. Just keep sitting.'

I ran over to Gwyn, and whispered to him. He spun round, at the same time taking a small bottle out of his jacket pocket. He fumbled in his top pocket as he ran back and produced a worn, tin spoon.

He pushed into the pew, and asked me to support Emrys's head, while he poured out a colourless liquid and forced it into the gasping man's mouth. Some dribbled down Emrys's chin, but most went in. Then, after he had put the cork back into the bottle, he stuck it down on a pew shelf, while he rolled up his raincoat and made a pillow.

We laid Emrys along the pew seat, while the other guests, suddenly aware that something was wrong, came thronging anxiously over to us.

Slowly, Emrys's face lost some of its agony, the breathing became more normal. I crouched in the narrow space beside him and chafed his hands anxiously. Someone lent a coat to put over him. The verger was asked to telephone the guest house and arrange for a doctor to be called.

Emrys's eyes had been tight closed, but as he relaxed he opened them and looked at me. 'Helen.'

As soon as he felt he could bear to be moved, two men in the party made a seat with crossed hands and carried him into the bus and laid him down on the back seat. Gwyn cradled his head, and I knelt by him and held him, so that he did not fall off. He lay quietly.

The bus driver manoeuvred the bus very carefully over the narrow lanes, and as soon as we reached the guest house, two of the staff came running out with a wooden chair with arms. Emrys was lifted from the bus into the chair, despite mild protests that he thought he could walk. He was not a heavy man and the two young men made short work of carrying him up the stairs and into his room. He was closely followed by a doctor carrying a black bag and by his anxious brother. I stood forlornly at the bottom of the stairs, and then reluctantly went to my room to wash before dinner.

Everybody in the dining room seemed to be talking about the fatal heart attacks they had witnessed, and I was very cast down, though Margaret did her best to cheer me up.

Gwyn did not come down to the meal, so when we had finished Margaret and I went into the hall and, after a moment's uncertainty on Margaret's part, went to the office to inquire if they had news.

We were told that while we were at dinner an ambulance had come and Mr Hughes and his brother had gone to a hospital in a nearby town. Margaret and I looked at each other, and then in silent consent went to the prayer meeting.

I did not sleep much. I was filled with a strange emotion such as I had not experienced before, a fear of the loss of a loved one.

The next morning, before breakfast, I plucked up enough courage to go myself to the office to inquire if they had news of Emrys. They had not, but the manager allowed me to use the telephone to inquire from the hospital how he was.

Mr Hughes was resting comfortably, I was told primly. He was not yet allowed visitors.

At breakfast I passed this information to Margaret. Despite my depression, I ate a huge breakfast and while still at table, said good-bye to Margaret, because she had to leave immediately in order to catch her train home. I went up to the bedroom and silently put my few belongings back into their paper bag, while the turmoil of the packing being done by the five mill girls went on around me. There was a strong smell of dirty washing and violet perfume, and I was glad to escape.

I said good-bye to the staff and to several other guests, and caught the train back to Liverpool and to reality.

Chapter twenty-six

The family were quite pleased to see me back and asked many questions, which I answered frankly. I told Mother about the Hughes brothers, and she made a little grimace with her mouth, and asked, 'They didn't touch you, did they?'

'Emrys held my hand,' I said.

She laughed in a deprecating way, and I was unaccountably incensed.

'They were very good to me,' I said defensively, and retreated to wash the dishes before I was provoked into saying more.

Such an excellent holiday gave me a lot more strength, and I formed the ambition of learning to type. The evening schools did not give courses in typing; my shorthand speed was rapidly increasing, but without a concomitant skill in typing, it was not much use to me.

I went to see Miriam in the attic. She very willingly allowed me to use her typewriter in the lunch hours and showed me how to manipulate the machine. She saved wastepaper so that I could use the back of it for practising. The three typists crammed into the little room took turns in instructing me how to set out letters, agendas and minutes. The head typist also showed me how to use the big Gestetner duplicating machine with its huge tubes of very black, very sticky ink.

Emrys was constantly in my mind and I daily hoped for a letter to say he was well again. But there was none. I told myself that I was such a small, unimportant person that perhaps I had been only someone to amuse him while he recuperated from his earlier heart attack. But I would see him again in my mind's eye, teasing, talking, laughing with me, and thus reassure myself that we had been really good companions and a true friendship had been formed.

At the end of the month, I plucked up courage, took a piece of copy paper from Miriam's store and, one lunch hour, wrote to the address he had given me, to inquire how he was.

Again, I began to watch for a letter, but still there was nothing. My new-found strength began to fade under the constant pressure of work at home, work at the office, work at night school, and the everlasting hunger. I fell into a quiet depression and found it hard to concentrate on my studies.

One hot sultry August day, when I arrived home to find the family, as usual, just finishing their evening meal, I was greeted by Mother with the information that my friend had died. She said it not unkindly, as she tossed an open letter across the table to me.

I slowly turned back into the hall and hung up my hat and coat. I did not want to touch the letter; I did not want to have the shocking news confirmed. I stood panting in the hall trying not to cry. People did not die; they got better from heart attacks, didn't they?

Mother was saying, 'Have a look at your letter.'

Reluctantly I picked it up. First I looked at the signature. Gwyn Hughes.

It began, 'Dear little Helen' and for a second I was tripping along beside a rushing river, and Emrys was saying, 'Be careful, little Helen. Don't fall in.'

Gwyn apologised for not writing to me earlier, but he had had so much to do that it was only now that he was able to attend to his personal correspondence.

Emrys had recovered sufficiently from his heart attack for the hospital doctor to say that he could make the journey back to Wales in a private car, if they broke the journey frequently enough for him to rest. At the moment of leaving the hospital, he had been stricken by another massive attack which had taken his life. His body had been taken home and had been buried beside those of his wife and his son, who had died when he was twelve.

Gwyn was sorry to have to send me such bad news. My companionship had been a great pleasure to both of them, and Emrys had been determined not to let the friendship lapse. He was going to write to me as soon as he returned to Wales.

With quivering hands, I put the letter back in the envelope. I was too shaken to complain about the letter's being opened. All I wanted to do was to go to bed and rest, shut myself out of life for a while.

Brian and Tony, those great companions, were staring at me uneasily. Probably death frightened them, too.

I smiled wryly at them. 'He was quite old,' I reassured them. 'It was natural.'

'I'm sorry,' said Father. 'They sound like very nice people. Very kind.'

I put the letter in my handbag. 'I will write to thank him,' I said.

'You should,' said Mother. 'Come and have your tea, dear.'

Fiona silently gave up her chair to me, and Alan passed over the bread and margarine. Mother brought me a small plate of lettuce and cold meat. For the first time that I could remember, I was aware of an aura of kindly sympathy throughout the family. Very slowly, in a dazed way I began to eat.

Chapter twenty-seven

I knew Emrys Hughes for only two weeks, but he left me a legacy which changed my whole life. He taught me that I was worthy of love and respect. He revealed to me that, given normal circumstances, I could be a cheerful, merry companion. He gave me self-respect, a belief in myself. This change in attitude did not reveal itself immediately because I was locked into circumstances beyond my control. But it was there, tucked away in the back of my mind to give me strength of purpose when the time came.

The raunchy cotton mill girls had also done something for me. I had not at first understood their conversation, because I did not know the words they used, but constant repetition soon made their meanings clear. They talked of nothing but sex, and their lurid discussions soon knitted together for me much that I knew subconsciously before. Then the reading of a great number of files and observation of the prostitutes in the streets greatly added to my understanding. One is supposed to be shaken by such revelations, but it all seemed quite normal to me and I accepted it without being disturbed. Perhaps because I was so starved, I had almost no feelings myself. My days were choked with work that had to be done, giving little time for contemplation of anything other than the next essay to be written, the next cup of tea to be provided.

I did not think of sex in connection with Emrys Hughes. He was a dear person, very careful of me, and I gave him the same kind of affection that I gave my grandmother, uninhibited and unthinking. Only years later, in the ripeness of womanhood, I realised that he might well have fallen for an innocent slip of a girl. He would not have been the first man to love someone thirty years younger than himself. But that last fortnight of his life was not wasted. It enriched mine immeasurably.

*

One of the more understanding ladies dressed in green overalls was a psychologist, a Mrs Croft, and, unlike the others, she would sometimes talk to me when I took her in a cup of tea at a time when she had no client with her. She knew that I attended night school and was learning shorthand. She asked me if I could teach another girl this subject.

The girl lived too far from the city to attend evening school. She could, however, take a lesson immediately upon finishing work and before going home. I could use Mrs Croft's husband's office as a place to give the lesson, and could charge about one shilling and sixpence each time.

So once a week, on an evening when there was no night school, I went to Mr Croft's office for an hour and gave a lesson to a languid, uninterested girl a little older than myself, while the cleaning staff mopped and dusted round us.

Probably because I was not a very good teacher, the girl quickly lost interest. But I earned enough money to enable me to put an advertisement in the *Liverpool Echo*, and acquire another pupil. A boy of about sixteen, suffering from epilepsy, asked to be taught at home. He was a very different kind of person, eager and enthusiastic. He practised assiduously and, by the time his parents moved with him to a milder climate, he was writing steadily at forty words per minute.

My parents approved of this tutoring, though Mother grumbled because I would not be available to help until late in the evening. I said that I proposed to keep the one shilling and sixpence a week that I was earning, towards buying lunches and some clothes.

At first, Mother frequently borrowed what I made, by riffling through my handbag and taking the money out. She never considered it necessary to pay it back. Finally, I made a stout little cotton bag to hold the precious pennies, and hung it round my neck by a piece of string. Once a week, I went to Woolworth's cafeteria at lunch time and bought a threepenny bowl of excellent soup and a roll. It was a treat to look forward to.

Before I thought of keeping my teaching money in a bag round my neck, and had managed to accumulate a few shillings, the shoes I had worn on holiday got to a point where there was so little sole left that I could not keep the pieces of cardboard from falling out. Finding shoes for all the children must have been a nightmare for Mother, and the best she could do for me was to give me her summer sandals which still had a little wear in them.

I woke up one morning to a black city suddenly made into a wonderland by an early fall of snow. I spent my last penny on a tram to work, but still my feet were sopping wet and freezing before I arrived at the office.

I sat down in the office kitchen, took off the sandals and wiped them with the floor cloth. Then I rubbed the stockinged toes with the same cloth.

The letters for hand delivery that morning were fortunately all for nearby offices, and I was just about to set out with them when the Cashier sent for me.

This forbidding lady always frightened me and she was not in the best of moods. She had a letter to be delivered to the Dental Hospital about a mile and a quarter away. It was still snowing, so I asked if I might take the tram.

'No,' she snapped. 'We haven't any money to waste on tram fares.'

By the time the local letters had been delivered, the snow was nearly up to my ankles and I was in real pain. Before setting out for the long trudge up the hill to the Dental Hospital, I sat down on an office stairway, took off the sandals and knocked the snow out of them, then brushed off the ice clinging to the stockings. I was weeping, and I wondered if I took the letter back to the office and refused to deliver it, I would be dismissed.

I decided that I probably would lose the job, and I dreaded this more than anything else. So up the hill I went through almost deserted streets, delivered the letter, and came down again at a stumbling run, crying all the way with pain in my feet. I envied Alan the new pair of shoes that had recently been bought for him. But he also got his feet wet that day.

Back at the office, I stripped off shoes and stockings filled a sink with water and, teetering on one toe, plunged each foot in turn into the hot water. Then I tried to dry them on the roller towel, an impossible feat. So I left a trail of water leading to the kitchen, while I went to dry them on the floor cloth.

As I put on the wet stockings again, I began to laugh shakily at the idea of the Presence surprising me with one foot caught in a roller towel. She was kind enough that, had she known about it, she would probably have been very upset at my being sent so far in such bad weather.

I was still shivering as I ran to make the tea and then fled up and down the eternal stone steps to deliver it, but probably the exercise helped to restore the circulation. I was left with only a very bad cold.

That lunch time, Miriam offered to lend me a portable typewriter for a week, so that I could practise at home. She was a member of the Communist Party and did all she could to attract other members. Another of the stenographers was an equally ardent member of the Roman Catholic Church and also keen on converts. So between the two of them, I received a lot of attention. Life was such a struggle for me, however, that I had neither time nor strength to consider their arguments and remained totally uncommitted.

The loan of the typewriter was most kindly meant

and I wanted to hug Miriam in gratitude. She brought it to the office the next day and I took it home, with some scrap paper, and put it in the empty front room. The children all wanted to try it, but I told them it had to be taken special care of because it was on loan. I joyfully practised far into the night, much to the irritation of Father, who could not sleep because of the steady tapping. I was myself always short of sleep, because I did my homework in the early mornings before the family got up, or late at night after they had gone to bed, provided that there was a penny to put in the gas meter to obtain light, or a stump of candle.

When I had finished my long practice, I returned the typewriter to the safety of the front room, put a penny from my handbag into the gas meter ready for the morning and crept up to bed. I was filled with hope that a good typing speed would help me to get a better job.

Chapter twenty-eight

The following evening I had to go to night school, so I was too busy to practise on the typewriter. On the third evening, I hurried through my work and then ran into the empty front room to fetch the machine.

There was no typewriter.

Perplexed, I looked in a built-in cupboard by the fireplace, but it held only the gas meter.

Mystified, I went back into the living room, where Mother was sitting by the fire reading the newspaper. Edward and Avril were playing on the coconut matting, squabbling over a few cigarette cards they had found.

'Mummy, did you move the typewriter from the front room?'

Mother looked up with studied casualness, and I knew instinctively that something was wrong.

'Yes, I did,' she said carefully.

'Well, where did you put it?' I asked impatiently. 'I want to practise.'

'It is not here.' Her cultivated voice was without expression.

The fearful apprehension in which I spent most of my life suddenly reached swamping proportions.

'Mother! What have you done with it? You haven't sold it, have you?'

'No.' She was looking at me with a kind of lazy indifference. I felt as if she had me impaled on a pin and that in the back of her mind she was enjoying the situation. My childish belief that parents always did the best they could for their offspring had long since vanished, and I was very frightened.

'Mother,' I whispered. 'What *have* you done with it? Are you teasing me – joking?'

'I never joke,' said Mother, and I realised that that was true.

She got up from her chair with a slow graceful movement, walked past me and into the hall. Through the open door, I watched her leisurely put on her hat and then her coat.

'Where is it, Mother?'

'In pawn.'

'Oh, my God! For how much?'

'Three pounds.'

I gasped. 'But I've got to return it in a couple of days!'

'Oh, don't worry. I'll get it out in due course.' She turned towards the front door.

'By Friday?'

'Oh, I doubt that.'

'Oh, Mummy!'

'Don't be so melodramatic,' she fumed irritably, as she opened the front door. 'You must make an excuse to keep it another week. It's time Avril and Edward were put to bed.'

The cold was thick in my head and my throat was so sore and constricted that I could hardly ask the next question.

'What shall I do if Miriam says she needs the machine?'

She snapped back angrily, 'That's your headache. You should be able to manage something like that.'

I stared speechlessly at her as she stepped out on to the pavement slamming the front door after her. All the horrors that could possibly befall me if the machine was not returned flew through my head. Accusations of theft, of court proceedings, loss of my job. I could tell Father, but what could he do? He had no money to speak of.

There was no one to help me. I wished that the dirty, linoleumed floor would open up and swallow me, so that I did not have to face poor Miriam.

My terror was so great that it blotted out everything else. I failed to hear instructions given to me in the office, and was constantly in trouble for forgetting small errands which the filing clerks pressed upon me. I forgot to take a voluntary worker a cup of tea. I accidently put a 'By Hand' letter into the post box; the firm it was addressed to telephoned to complain about having to pay the postage. I carried a big tea tray carelessly through a doorway and knocked the spouts off two teapots. I stood, appalled, while tea gushed all over the floor, and the Cashier ranted that I would have to pay for new teapots. I nearly laughed at her. At night school, I sat at my desk and saw and heard nothing. The essays and assignments set me remained undone.

'Whatever is the matter, Helen?' each teacher, in turn, demanded testily.

Miriam reluctantly agreed to allow me to keep the typewriter for another week.

At home, I moved like a zombie through the usual routine of baby-sitting, shopping, cooking, cleaning, washing, ironing. The children were used to my being quiet, except when embroiled in a fight with my parents or a rare spate with Alan or Fiona, so I doubt if they noticed much change. Father lived in his dream world, went most evenings to the library and on Saturday and Sunday went out for a drink with a colleague. I saw no point in asking Father's help; it would spark another family row. Only Mother knew, and she made no reply when I pestered her to redeem the machine.

I had never considered that children might love their mothers. I always feared mine.

I think that sometimes, when I was little, Mother felt guilty at pushing me on to Grandma or to Edith, and it was then that she would send for me. She would listen to my reading or give me a sweet and ask me about school. But she did not really hear me when I replied, and I would thankfully rush back to Edith or close my eyes and look forward to the next visit to Grandma's house.

At the end of the second week, Miriam said she needed the typewriter. Her rich brown crown of shining hair swung round her pixielike face, as she looked up at me with such a friendly grin that I wanted to cry.

'I'll bring it in on Monday,' I promised, my voice strained with the cold and sheer terror.

At home, Father was out, and I had a fearsome row

with Mother to no purpose, and retired to bed crying hysterically.

On Tuesday, Miriam, her expression a little puzzled, inquired again.

I apologised for forgetting to bring the machine in the rush of getting to work. On Thursday and Friday, I muttered the same apologies. She just nodded and looked curiously and unsmilingly at me. Undoubtedly, she had begun to worry about her prized possession.

I was saved from having to face her on Saturday morning. One Saturday each month was free, and I stayed at home and did the washing.

Dressed in an old cotton frock, I was carefully washing my work skirt in the kitchen sink, when there was a polite rap on the iron door knocker.

Mother was cutting bread and margarine for tea, so, with hands still dripping, I went into the empty front room and peeped through the piece of net curtaining we had pinned across the windows.

Standing on the pavement looking up at the decrepit brick house was Miriam.

I flitted back to the kitchen.

'Mother!' I whispered in a panic. 'It's Miriam! She must have come for the typewriter. What am I going to do?'

Mother looked up from her bread cutting, knife poised in mid-air.

'Don't answer the door,' she said simply.

'But she must have come all the way over from the north end of town specially.'

'I said, "don't answer".'

I wrung my hands, as I hissed back, 'But, Mummy. . .'

She was implacable. 'Don't answer.'

I was panting with fright and stared at her helplessly for a minute. Then I said angrily in a normal voice, 'I *will* answer. I can't bear it any more. I will tell her exactly what has happened.' My voice rose in hysteria. 'I just can't endure it any longer.'

Fiona, the only other person at home, came in from the lavatory in the back yard. She stared at us in scared apprehension.

Miriam rapped again, louder. I started for the living room through which I would have to pass to reach the front passage.

'Oh, no, my lady.' Mother dropped her knife, swiftly slammed the door and put her foot against it. She glared at me. 'How dare you?'

I stopped. I wanted to strike her to make her move, but it was so alien to me that I could not.

In a fever of fear, I shouted, 'I will tell them in the office on Monday and then they will know you stole it.'

Mother went white. 'You would not dare to tell such a lie,' she retorted, as the knocker sounded once again.

But I did not care what happened, as long as the intolerable burden was removed from me, and I replied determinedly. 'It is not a lie and I certainly would dare.'

'All right. I will speak to Miriam. You remain here.' She was bristling with anger.

She opened the living room door and marched through to the front of the house.

I clung to the kitchen table, hardly able to stand, while the sound of the front door opening and then Mother's delicate voice echoed through the house.

Mother and Miriam had not met before, so Miriam first explained who she was and then asked politely if she could have the machine back, because she had some work to do on it. Mother said enthusiastically how delighted she was to meet her and how grateful she was for her kindness to me. I closed my eyes and prayed, wondering what she would say next.

The well-bred voice was explaining that she herself had ventured to use the machine yesterday. Unfortunately, one of the letters had fallen off and needed soldering on again, so she had taken it up to town to have it repaired.

'Oh, dear,' exclaimed Miriam. 'Where did you take it?'

'Um, you know that place on Dale Street? I took it there. They said it would be ready on Tuesday.'

Miriam sounded very relieved, as she replied, 'Oh, that's not too bad. I could pick it up myself.'

Mother's voice chimed in with measured charm. 'Oh, I won't hear of it. I must pay for it. I will arrange for Helen to bring it into the office on Wednesday. I am so sorry that up to now she has been so delinquent about returning it. I will make sure that this time she does not forget.'

There was a mumble of polite, friendly argument, then good-byes were said, and the front door was softly closed.

I was so shaken that I wanted to vomit.

'What was that about?' asked Fiona, as she took her skipping rope off a hook on the back door.

I did not reply for a moment, and then I said wearily, 'It's so complicated, Fi, I can't explain it. But everything is O.K. now.'

Chapter twenty-nine

Mother had barely shut the front door, when the string on the latch was pulled and the door again swung open. Brian and Tony came bursting in from playing football in the street. They were excited because it had begun to snow heavily, and they thought that later on they might be able to make a snowman. They were followed almost immediately by Avril and Baby Edward, who had toddled down to Granby Street together, to buy a pint of milk; the milkman had refused to deliver any more until his bill was paid. Giggling together triumphantly, they handed me the bottle.

Since the children were there, Mother said nothing to me, but, as she picked up the bread knife again, her contemptuous look spoke volumes. Feeling wretched, I returned to the sink full of washing.

As I was hanging the garments over a piece of string strung across the kitchen, Father and Alan came through the back door, laughing and shaking the snow off themselves.

I must tell Daddy, I thought. I simply have to. But not now, because of the children. Mother will turn on me, the minute I open my mouth. But three pounds is a huge sum to raise. How does Mother imagine she is going to do it?

Mother was very quiet during tea. By silent

consent nothing was said about Miriam before the children.

I had to give a shorthand lesson that evening, so immediately after tea I prepared a protesting Edward for bed. I borrowed Fiona's macintosh from her to put over my cotton dress, because my skirt was not dry and my own very light macintosh was neither windproof nor waterproof. I would have to talk to Daddy in the morning. With a quick glance at the clock, I snatched up my shorthand books and ran to catch a tram outside the Rialto Cinema. To reach my pupil's home, it was necessary to take a tram to the Pier Head and another one out again to his district. There was no question of being able to walk the distance in a reasonable time.

The snow was coming down in great fleecy flakes and my feet were soaked before I reached the end of our street. The bright lights of the cinema seemed to be floating amid the flakes, and a drift was forming across its curved front steps. The clumsy trams looked like glittering ghosts as they churned their way slowly along Catherine Street. Few people were about, and for a second I considered turning back. But I needed money so badly that when my tram arrived, I swung on to it without hesitation.

'Lousy night,' remarked the conductor as I tendered the fare.

At the Pier Head, the wind was driving the snow in whirling sweeps across the stone sets, almost obliterating the Royal Liver Building and the squat Cunard Building. The Church of our Lady and St Nicholas was lost amid the white downpour. As if from nowhere, the sounds of the fog horns and the harsh bells to guide the ferry boats came floating round my head. One or two shadowy people scurried past me.

Surrounding the tram superintendent was a tight knot of drivers and conductors, red ears sticking out from navy blue caps and glowing cigarettes drooping from their mouths. They were arguing about stopping the service. I was shivering, and clutched the macintosh collar round my neck to stop the snow trickling down inside, as I waited for their decision. The wind from the river seemed to penetrate my bones.

The superintendent vanished in search of the telephone.

I blew my nose on a square of newspaper, then shoved my bare hands into my mac pockets in an effort to keep them from freezing. The heavy flakes clung to my hair and I brushed a rosette of snow off my bun. The drivers and conductors climbed back into their respective trams to get out of the wind. I did not dare to follow one of them for fear I missed my own tram, which had not yet arrived.

Long before I saw the tram I needed, I could hear the driver pinging its bell with one foot, as he edged the great vehicle slowly round the curve of Mann Island. Between the sharp pings of the bell came the sound of the slap of the river water around the floating dock behind me, the sound of the Mersey which lay between Grandma and me. For a moment, I felt like chancing my tram fares on a ferry fare instead and running away to her.

'Don't be a fool,' I told myself sharply. 'You haven't got the fare for the bus on the other side – and an eight mile walk in this storm is impossible.'

The supervisor, bustling with importance, came towards the newly arrived tram. The driver stepped down to meet him; he did not want to take the tram out again. The supervisor irately pointed out that on his return journey he normally picked up men coming off a night shift in an outlying factory. After some argument, the driver reluctantly climbed on to his platform, and I thankfully clambered into the back, shaking myself like a collie dog. I sat down on the wooden bench which ran the whole length of the car, bent over and lifted an almost solid crown of snow from the top of my head. It splashed all over the ridged floor as I dropped it. The interior of the vehicle was comfortingly warm, but I continued to shiver and my feet were bitterly cold. I was the only outgoing passenger and I stared glumly at the empty bench opposite, until the conductor came to collect my fare.

The driver slammed open the intervening door, letting in a great gust of snow-laden air. He shouted down the length of the car to the conductor that they would be lucky if they saw their beds that night. He was not going to be responsible if the bloody tram got stuck; he'd told the bastard back there that they would never make it up the hill. These remarks did not cheer me up. The tram was already far behind schedule and I would be very late for the lesson.

At Pembroke Place the points of the track were solid with ice and did not yield to the driver's poking at them with a metal bar. The conductor climbed down and a committee of two was held over them. Then, shaking themselves free of snow, they climbed back in again. The driver eased the brake off and let the tram roll slowly backwards down the hill for a few yards. Then he took the line up London Road. We were off the proper route, but not so far that I would not be able to run to my pupil's house.

As we crawled along, the thin, underclad conductor came into the body of the tram and closed the back door. He sat in the far corner from me, silently smoking cigarette after cigarette.

I was heavy with the cold which I had caught nearly three weeks earlier and had failed to shake off. As the chill from my waiting at the Pier Head wore off, I gradually began to feel stiflingly hot, and I almost envied the driver out in the wind. My head ached abominably and I laid it against the cold windowpane and closed my eyes. I suffered greatly from headaches, partly, I think, from eye strain, so another one was nothing to worry about.

After what seemed an interminable time of grinding noise as the tram laboured onwards, I was jerked awake. The tram had stopped. The lights were still on and the motor was throbbing.

The driver pushed open his door and came in, puffing and blowing, his face nearly purple between his peaked cap and great muffler. The conductor looked up.

The driver addressed me.

'Can't go no further, Miss,' he announced.

'God spare us,' exclaimed the conductor, and

threw his cigarette butt angrily on to the floor. 'Where are we?' he asked.

I picked up my wet shorthand books from beside me, as the driver replied, 'West Derby Road, near Green Lane. I thought I could work my way round, like, to me proper route. But I couldn't turn at Shiel Road like I hoped. Had no luck at all. And now there's two abandoned trams on the track ahead of us. I can't see no sign of drivers or conductors.'

West Derby Road! I was miles from where I should have been and at least three miles from home. I looked in alarm at the two men discussing what they should do. They seemed to be fuzzy round the edges. I got up from the seat. My legs wobbled, and I sat down again quickly. I was suddenly afraid of the bitter cold outside.

The driver said, 'We'd better all get home as best we can. If I can find a phone box on the way, I'll phone the boss to say where the tram is.' He took off his big scarf, as he spoke, and shook a shining cascade of snow off it. 'Could try taking the bloody thing in in the morning, when I'll be able to see better.'

Trams can be driven from either end. They do not have to be turned, so I asked, 'Couldn't you drive it back again to the Pier Head?'

'What for, luv? There's nothing there but wind and water.'

The conductor peered ineffectually through a bit of window he had rubbed clear of steam. 'Snow's so deep, we'd probably stick anyway. Best get home, like you say.'

I nodded and the pain jabbed through my head. How was I to find my way through a maze of narrow streets, snow-choked and deserted? Yet there seemed nothing else to do. Once the driver turned off the power, the tram would quickly become very cold indeed.

'Do you know how I can get to the Rialto Cinema?' I asked.

They looked at me appalled. 'Eee, you do have a way to go,' exclaimed the driver.

Again, a committee of two was formed. The driver lived in Holt Road, the conductor in Old Swan, which in normal circumstances was no great walk from where we were stranded. The conductor decided to leave us. He turned up his overcoat collar, said 'Ta-ra, well,' very dolefully, cautiously stepped down into the street and plodded away into the night.

The driver, sighing heavily, decided to drive the tram back along the route he had come to the nearest point to his home street or until the vehicle stalled. This would help me, too, and he said he could direct me home from where he lived. He floundered outside again and succeeded with difficulty in reversing the trolley on the overhead wires, and then heaved himself into the rear of the tram to drive it.

He left the communicating door slightly ajar, so that he could talk to me and I moved up to the end of the bench closest to it. We sailed slowly down the same side of the street up which we had travelled. I hoped we would not hit another vehicle which might be coming towards us. There seemed, however, to be no other thing moving in the city, and our tram finally refused to go any further after reaching Shiel Road.

The driver slammed the vehicle's doors shut, and took my arm. Together we struggled on foot along Shiel Road, while the wind blew the snow into our faces, down our necks and up our coat sleeves. The driver had boots, an overcoat, a cap, a scarf and gloves. I had on a cotton dress, a macintosh and a second-hand pair of walking shoes which I had bought from the pawnbroker for two shillings. My head and hands were bare, and rayon stockings did not offer much protection. I was also very thin, with no proper layer of fat to help ward off the cold. I regretted bitterly ever having set out.

By the time we found the driver's brick, terrace house, with his wife peeping anxiously through the tiny bay window, the wind had eased and the snow was thinning.

His wife invited me in to rest and shelter for a while, but my mind seemed to be fogged up and all I could think about was the desperate need to get home and into bed. Stupidly, I said that the snow was easing and I could manage to walk home.

She nodded doubtfully at me, as her husband stamped about behind her in the narrow hallway, and she closed the door slowly as I moved away.

Durning Road to Tunnel Road, from dim gas lamp to dim gas lamp, alternately freezing and perspiring, I struggled on, through totally deserted streets. This was not a district of private cars, but here and there a van or truck had been abandoned and

219

snowdrifts were rising round them. Each window sill I passed had a neat traycloth of snow on it, each doorstep its unbroken drift.

I was beginning to think that I would have to knock at the nearest door and ask for shelter, when I suddenly found myself at the junction of Upper Parliament Street and Smithdown Road. And through the unearthly silence, came unexpectedly the distant rumble of a tram. I looked quickly down Smithdown Road from where the sound seemed to come. I saw the electricity spit and its reflection flash across the snow as its trolley crossed a wire. I half stumbled, half ran towards it.

The driver – there was no conductor – was astonished to have a passenger suddenly emerge from the storm. He stopped, and let me on through the front of the tram.

'Eh, Miss. You must be frozen. Where you tryin' to get to?'

'The Rialto,' I gasped, as I felt down my chest and eased out my little money bag, to get a penny from it. A pain like a knife wound was shooting through my back and my throat was swelling in its old threatening manner.

'Eh, you don't have to pay t' fare,' he said, through the slightly ajar front door, near which I had thankfully taken a seat. 'I'm trying to get that far for me own sake. I got a flat in Catherine. But I reckon points will be frozen, so I won't be able to turn.' He jerked his head to indicate the way he had come, and added, 'It was bloody awful back there. I let me conductor off by his house.'

I nodded dumbly. In the warmth of the tram, my head was whirling as the snowflakes had been, and all I could think about was home.

The snow had stopped when, about fifteen minutes later, I pulled the string on our door latch and stumbled in, into my father's arms.

Chapter thirty

I have a dim remembrance of Father rolling off my stockings in front of the fire and putting my feet into a basin of luke-warm water, to restore the circulation; of Mother holding a cup of scalding hot tea to my lips, and of being surprised at the anxiety in her pale blue eyes. Then I was in bed with Edward's hot water bottle pressed to my back and Father was cursing as he tried to make a fire in the bedroom fireplace.

Faces came and went in the candlelight. Or was it sunlight? Medicine was forced down my throat, a poultice applied to my back. Fiona helped to hold me on a chamberpot placed on the bed. Once it seemed to me that Edith was there and I called out to her, but she faded away. I dreamed that Minerva came down from her seat on the top of the town hall and shook her spear at me for being so foolish. Then there was a great nightmare during which I was arguing with the pawnbroker about the return of the typewriter. I kept shouting at him that he must give it to me because it was stolen property. I had long spasms of coughing, when all of me seemed wracked with aches and pains. I was dreadfully hot and kept throwing off the bed-clothes, but they were always tucked round me again.

Then, quite suddenly, I was shivering in the light of the pale Liverpool sun coming through the bedroom window. My feet were sticking out from under the coverings, and I pulled them up close to me. The movement sent a shooting pain through them. A cold hot water bottle lay at my side and I tried to push it away, but somehow my hands would not obey so I lay still.

After a little while, I opened my eyes again and turned my head. A small fire was smouldering in the grate, and, in the double bed on the other side of the room lay Brian. He was tucked up tightly in a pile of bedding and coats. His hair stuck up like the hairs of a shaving brush and the face beneath was yellow with two bright red spots on the cheekbones.

I tried to ask him what had happened, but when I moved, such a pain shot through my head from both ears, and my throat seemed so swollen, that I barely got the first word out.

He seemed to understand, and one small, chil-blained hand crept out of his covering and he pointed to his throat. He managed a wry little smile.

Mother came slowly in. Her feet dragged, as she came over to me. Without make-up and without her hair combed, she looked faded and pinched. She must have been exhausted, after having two invalids to care for, particularly since I would normally have taken a lot of the load from her.

She saw with obvious relief that I was awake. To allay the pain, I lay perfectly still while she put her hand on my forehead to check the temperature.

'How are you feeling?'

I tried to smile. 'Ears hurt – and throat and legs,' I croaked. 'Brian?'

Mother nodded. 'He has quinsy, poor boy. He is going into hospital this afternoon, to have it cut.' The lines on her face deepened. Brian was one of her favourite children.

'Where is he going?'

'The Ear, Nose and Throat Hospital.'

Very carefully, I turned my face towards the other bed. Despite his illness, Brian's eyes crinkled up cheerfully at me.

For a long time, I lay looking at the cracked, grey ceiling, trying not to weep with weakness and pain, because crying only constricted the already painfully tight throat. Mother brought both Brian and me a cup of tea and supported us in turn as we drank.

The doctor came in the afternoon and dispatched Brian, still stoically cheerful, in an ambulance to the hospital. Then he turned to me.

'I was beginning to think I'd have to send you in, too,' he said, as he probed round my neck with his fingers.

I smiled weakly. 'What have I had?'

'You've had a nasty attack of bronchitis – in fact, it is still with you – but I think you will mend now. You also managed a bad dose of 'flu. And now we have to tackle your throat and ears.'

I nodded, while he took a camel hair brush out of his bag and a bottle of tannic acid, so that he could paint my throat. After he had done that, he put drops in both ears. He was very gentle, his handsome young face filled with concern. Afterwards, I learned that he did not charge for his visits to Brian, since he was already in the house to see me. Brian's hospital stay would be covered by charitable contributions to the hospital, he told Mother. He came every day, twice, to paint my throat and check my ears.

All I could eat for a while was a cup of Oxo with bread mashed into it or a cup of tea, but I slept a lot.

Two days after my delirium left me, I remembered Miriam's typewriter. I lay sobbing quietly for hours in great fear about it, while Mother did an afternoon stint in a department store.

Father was home first. I had heard Fiona come in, followed by the other children, but she was making the tea, judging by the sounds that floated up the stairs, and had not come to see me. Father came straight upstairs and still had his hat in his hand as he sat down on the bed, careful not to shake me.

'Well, how's my girl?'

'Not bad,' I whispered.

He patted my hand, and I asked him eagerly, 'Daddy, do you know about the typewriter?'

He looked grim, as he said that he did.

'Were you able to get it back? Has Miriam got it?' It seemed as if my whole life hung on the answer.

He gave a little snort, with a hint of laughter in it. 'Yes, dear. She has.'

'Thank God,' I muttered. 'Thank God.' The burden was off me.

He sat staring sombrely at the empty fireplace – we had run out of coal. After a minute, I asked huskily how he had done it.

'Well, your Mother had applied for a five pound cheque to buy some clothes for the boys – and the finance company granted it. So we bought everything we could on it and pawned the lot. And we didn't pay the rent, so that made enough. Your Mother took the machine into the office – and I understand that Miriam was very nice to her.' He sighed heavily, and then said, 'Don't worry any more. You should have told me immediately it happened. I doubt if I would have known about it at all, if you had not shouted your head off over it while you were in delirium.' He looked down at me and laughed suddenly. 'There was quite a rumpus.'

I could imagine the row there must have been between Mother and him, and I grinned back at him.

'And I was out of it all,' I chuckled. My throat hurt and I stopped suddenly. 'It's a dreadful load of debt.'

'Nothing new,' he said, with the same sort of optimism that Alan sometimes displayed. 'You are not to worry. Just get well.'

'How long have I been ill?' I asked.

'Eight days.'

'When can I get up?'

'It will be some time yet.'

I laughed again, this time a little more carefully. 'Fiona still has to hold me on the chamberpot – so I suppose it will be a while.' Then I began to cough and to wince with pain in my chest and head. The smoke from his cigarette had got into my throat.

One day, the doctor asked Mother to refrain from smoking in the bedroom. She was very offended and railed against him as soon as he had gone. He had also lectured her on the necessity for getting some weight back on to both Brian's and my wasted bodies. He ordered cream, butter, potatoes, fresh vegetables, liver and eggs – and rest, lots of rest and fresh air for both of us.

Mother listened, and bowed her head politely from time to time, as he urged her quite passionately to stuff us with food. But when she had quietly closed the front door on him and had returned to the bedroom to give me a dose of cough mixture, she first fumed about his rudeness in asking her not to smoke, and then said crossly, 'And where does he think I will get the money from for cream?'

Tears of weakness forced themselves through crunched up eyelids, as I lay back on the pillow. I remembered the slice of bread for breakfast, the lack of lunch until I had managed to buy myself a bowl of soup or a roll and butter, the tiny plate of dinner kept from the hot meal Mother made either at lunch time or teatime, according to her work schedule. She did not eat much herself, but I was still growing; my needs were at least as great as Fiona's. I thought of Alan, able to go to the cinema on the strength of his pocket money, of the lunch he carried each day, of his new shoes and his tram fares. Why could not I have had the same?

And the answer seemed obvious. Because you are a girl old enough to be more useful at home than at work; a girl, moreover, whose very existence was resented from the day of her birth.

People, least of all parents, do not analyse their attitudes to children; and I am sure Father and Mother saw me only as a recalcitrant, disobedient offspring who had to be brought to heel. Their lives had been ruined and they were too exhausted to think their children's problems through. Mother used quantities of aspirin to sedate herself and Father, when he got the chance, vanished off for a drink. And they both smoked incessantly. They had neither time nor inclination to give sober, careful thought to what was happening to me.

Mother did, however, begin to bring me plenty of bread and margarine and big bowls of porridge with a little sugar and milk. But a great lassitude enveloped me. After a few mouthfuls, the throat seemed choked and I could not eat any more. Frequent small helpings were difficult for her to arrange because she worked a half-day on most week days, and she was herself tired to death.

Fiona helped me to use the chamberpot and she and Mother washed me. At first I accepted these attentions with about as much response as a rag doll would give. Then, as I grew a little stronger, the wells of gratitude were loosed and I would thank them effusively for every service, however small.

I began to worry that such a long absence would mean dismissal from my job. And how long would it take me to get strong enough to face those awful stone stairs and heavy trays again? And my night school work would be weeks behind.

I asked Fiona to bring me my text books and I lay with them on the bedclothes, too weak, too tired to lift them up and read them. When Mother went to the library, she very kindly brought me a pile of novels and these were the first books that I read, as I grew a little stronger and was able to sit up.

As the fear that I might die receded, Mother began to get impatient with my slow recovery. She was weary, weary beyond words, after coping with Brian's and my sickness, her own periodic jobs and all the tasks that I normally did. Fiona had been pressed into service, but Fiona was as good as Mahatma Gandhi at practising passive resistance; she had no intention of inheriting my domestic shoes. She learned quickly that trade union habit of working to rule. And who could be angry with such a gentle, helpless, blue-eyed beauty? None of us could.

When Brian returned from hospital, and, after a week's convalescence at home, was allowed to return to school, Mother seemed to feel that I should automatically have recovered as well.

I was unable to oblige, though our patient doctor had managed to bring down the inflammation in my throat, and the abscesses in my ears had burst and were healing. I was also able to sit on a chair, though I found a hard wooden one difficult to sit on because I had no fat on my buttocks.

Christmas was nearly upon us, though I had given no thought to preparing gifts and my parents had not mentioned it, when Fiona brought a letter up to me. Though the letter was addressed to me, it had been opened. It was from the Presence.

The Presence announced that she was very concerned that I had been so ill, and she would call to see me at three o'clock in two days' time.

The thought of such an important visitor as my employer coming into our bedroom threw me into a panic. What would she think of the stuffy, dirtiness of it, of the lack of bedspreads, even enough blankets? How would she regard a room furnished only with two beds, a candlestick, a wooden chair and an unscoured chamberpot? She was a gentlewoman, I reminded myself. She would be horrified.

'What shall I do?' I asked Mother when, later, she brought me a cup of Oxo.

'I think you had better see her downstairs,' said Mother. 'The doctor said you can get dressed for a little while tomorrow, so you can probably get down the stairs all right.'

I agreed fervently. If Mother tidied up the living room it would look much better than the bedroom did.

'How long did they pay my wages for, Mummy? Did they send any?'

'Oh, yes. They're still paying them. A money order comes every week. I cash it at the post office.'

'That's awfully kind of them,' I said.

'Well, they're a charity. They should be charitable,' Mother said, with considerable venom in her voice. She picked up my medicine bottle and shook it.

The sudden elation in me died at her remark. I shivered. How cold charity could be.

As I sipped the scalding Oxo, I told myself that I was stupid, inept, untrained and deserved the impatience of the filing clerks and Mr Ellis, the irritability of the Cashier who had the unenviable task of making the charity's ends meet. Two of the social workers, the ladies of the green overalls, had, at my first Christmas with them, given me gifts, one of sweets, the other of a bottle of lavender, which I had promptly used as gifts for Mother and Fiona; so they knew I existed. There were days, however, when I wondered if I was really a person to the staff or whether I was just an inefficient piece of machinery. Mother had never regarded her servants as people; perhaps they thought of me like that.

I sighed, and dismissed the depressing subject. Anyone as unwashed, smelly, ugly and generally repulsive as me, I assured myself, was bound to suffer the opprobrium of those who could afford hot water and soap.

But the Presence realised I was a person. She had apparently ordered wages to be sent to me, and now she was going to call on me. She had sent me on a miraculous holiday which had given me the affection of Emrys Hughes, draper, during his last few weeks on earth.

At the thought of Emrys, tears of weakness began to flow. The battle to survive seemed too great to be borne and I wished I was with him.

'What are you crying for?' asked Mother. 'Come along, now. Take your medicine.'

Chapter thirty-one

Mother seemed anxious that we should make a good impression on the Presence; and on the day of her visit, she brought the tin basin from the kitchen and washed me all over with warm water. She had ironed my work skirt and she lent me one of her own blouses to wear. I was too weak to endure having my hair washed, so she combed it out and pinned it back from my face with a hair clip. All the time my heart went pit-a-pat at the thought of facing my formidable employer, and I was glad to rest before Mother supported me down the stairs.

To my surprise, she opened the front room door instead of the living-room door. Obediently, I tottered into the room and stared, unbelievingly, around me.

A small fire blazed in the hearth and gave a pleasant glow in a room made dark by an overcast afternoon. A pretty beige and green rug covered the floor; the windows were draped with pale green silky curtains. In front of the fire stood a new, beige settee, and at either side was a matching easy chair. In the window was a softly shining bureau. Over the mantelpiece hung a glittering, plate glass mirror. Reflected in it was a water colour painting hanging on the opposite wall. The picture was one painted for Mother when she was a young girl, and she had snatched it up when leaving our home; it was all she had of our earlier, more prosperous life, and she had never pawned it.

'Good Heavens!' I exclaimed. I was so startled that my weak legs gave way and I sat down suddenly on the settee.

'It looks nice, doesn't it?' said Mother, her face glowing. 'It's a little bare yet, but we'll soon add some more pieces. They delivered it on the Monday after you were taken ill.'

I replied truthfully that it looked extremely nice. I had more sense than to start a fight regarding the other ideas which shot into my mind. 'It's charming,' I added.

'I wasn't sure whether to choose beige curtains or green ones. But the green brocade seemed such good quality that I bought those.'

'They look lovely,' I assured her. 'Thanks for making a fire here.' My head was whirling with the effort I had made to get dressed and come downstairs, and my chest felt constricted and painful with the effort not to burst into helpless tears.

Mother smiled. 'I'll just go and tidy myself before your visitor arrives. It's fortunate that I did not have any work today.'

She closed the door quietly behind her, and I leaned back against the new upholstery. Mother was an intelligent, well-educated woman, but when I looked around me I doubted her sanity.

How many shillings each week was this new extravagance going to drain from us? I wondered. And if they felt compelled to buy something for the house, why not start with blankets and sheets or towels? Our beds still lacked the basic necessities to keep us warm and clean – and they had gone out and bought a drawing room full of furniture. I sobbed inside, not daring to cry aloud. And how much longer was I to go hungry – and to a lesser degree the other children, too – until the damned stuff was paid for? I knew that we had not yet finished paying for the furniture that had been repossessed. Would they never learn to be practical? I whimpered in feeble anger.

There was a quiet knock at the front door, and I hastily dashed errant tears away and sniffed. I had not got a handkerchief.

There was the sound of soft, refined voices in the hall, a familiar, slightly shuffling step. I eased myself round, with some difficulty, to face my employer as she entered. Somehow she did not look so awesome in these surroundings – just a frail, small, elderly lady with a genuine look of concern on her face, as she held out a little gloved hand to be shaken.

'How do you do?' I inquired politely.

Her eyes looked dreadfully tired, but she said, with a little smile, 'Very well, thank you. And how are you?'

'Better, thank you,' I managed to gulp.

Mother asked her to sit down on one of the easy chairs, and she did so. She loosened the fur collar of her dark winter coat, arranged her black handbag on her knee and crossed her ankles neatly.

Mother swished down into the other easy chair, and the Presence looked me up and down earnestly.

'You seem to have been very ill,' she said. 'You have lost a lot of weight.'

I nodded nervous agreement. I wanted to lie down, but did not dare to move.

'Has the doctor told you yet when you will be fit for work?'

Mother intervened. 'This is her first venture downstairs, so I imagine it will be a few weeks before she can do much walking.'

'I imagine so.' The Presence continued to gaze thoughtfully at me. I had the feeling she could have given a police description of me after such an intense scrutiny.

There was an embarrassed silence, finally broken by Mother, who inquired, 'Would you like a cup of tea? You must be cold after coming so far. Helen usually has a cup at this time.'

The Presence was drawing off her leather gloves. She glanced up at Mother, who had risen from her chair. 'I would enjoy one very much. Thank you.'

That got rid of Mother for a few minutes, which I had had an instinctive feeling the Presence wanted to do. She smoothed her wrinkled gloves between absent-minded fingers, as she looked round the room. I noticed that her thin face had fine, premature lines round the eyes and at each side of the firm mouth. She wore no powder or lipstick, and she had the quiet, deft movements of a nun.

'This is a pleasant place for you to sit, isn't it? I am happy that your family seems to be getting on to its feet again.'

I wanted to lean forward and put my head into her tweed-covered lap and bellow tearfully that, in my opinion, the whole room was an outrage to reason. Instead, I whispered, 'Yes, it is a nice room.'

'You have been with us for two years, now,' she said with sudden briskness. It was a statement, not a question.

I nodded, and she sighed as if the fact was cause for woe.

'We need an extra girl in the Registry Office, to look after the index cards and to help with the filing. Such a girl would have to relieve the telephone operator at lunch time. I understand that you can now manage the switchboard; and it has been decided to give the new position to you. Er – Mr Ellis is agreeable to this.' She looked at me expectantly, a suggestion of a twinkle in her eyes.

The sense of overwhelming relief I felt was so great that, at first, I could not speak. I opened my mouth and no words came. A promotion! No more making tea or having to go out in the snow, and less running up and down stairs.

'Oh, thank you,' I finally gasped, with such sincerity that she really smiled this time.

'Your salary would be twelve shillings and sixpence, payable monthly.'

I was in ecstasy. 'That would be splendid,' I whispered. I wanted to shout it from the rooftops, dance in the street. Life was beginning to move forward at last.

'You can tell your parents about it yourself,' she added, in a tone of voice which hinted something which I did not at first grasp. Then, as I heard the rattle of teacups in the back room, I realised that she was being very forebearing. In a period when children of the middle classes remained children until their majority, it would have been quite possible that she would discuss this promotion with Mother before telling me, particularly as she herself belonged to a still earlier generation. She had, however, left me the choice of telling my parents about the salary increase, or not. Did she, I wondered, understand something of the misery I was going through?

'You are very kind,' I said warmly.

Because our crockery was chipped and ugly and we lacked many essentials, like milk jugs, Mother brought the Presence a cup of tea with milk already in it, and proffered the cheap, glass sugar basin with its tin spoon.

The tea was graciously accepted and consumed, the bad weather discussed and good wishes expressed for my early recovery.

'We will see if we can arrange another holiday this summer,' the Presence promised, as Mother took her cup from her.

Mother made no comment. Her smile was thin and polite. With a jolt, I wondered if she would try to keep me at home again, on the excuse of chronic ill-health. Perhaps I would never return to the office. Perhaps she was just willing to accept the payment of my salary as long as the organisation was prepared to pay it.

I must have gone even whiter at the idea, because the Presence said suddenly, 'Helen is exhausted. I must go.'

Hands were shaken, and Mother showed my

kind visitor out. I thankfully lay down on the settee.

If Mother and Father could buy over a hundred pounds' worth of sitting room furniture, I meditated bitterly, then they did not need the extra half-a-crown a week I would be earning. I desperately needed to be able to buy soup for lunch each day, instead of once a week. I needed shoes and second-hand woollens to keep me warm. The money I was already giving to Mother was more than adequate for the small amount of food I received, for the coal and gas I shared, and for a small contribution to the rent. I determined that Mother should have the next rise in pay I received, but not this one.

'And if you think I am going to stay at home, you can think again,' I muttered to myself acidly.

Mother had been quite patient while nursing me, but, from sad experience, I doubted if that patience would extend past the day I managed to walk about.

Chapter thirty-two

The doctor feared that the infection of my ears would cause a loss of hearing, and he insisted that I should see a specialist. So, a few days before Christmas, Mother managed to bundle me on to a tram, and we went to the Ear, Nose and Throat Hospital.

Since I was very weak, we arrived early, in the hope of being seen without much delay by the specialist, who donated his services to the hospital.

When I looked up at the building, it seemed to touch the pale blue sky. Its tall, narrow windows, the stonework beautifully carved by long dead masons, seemed to be slender fingers pointing upwards. Mother propped me against the wall, as close as she could get to the pollution-blackened doorway, where a shabby crowd awaited the opening of the Out-patients' Department. A cold wind fluttered the stained raincoats of the men and the bundly overcoats of the women, some of whom hugged beshawled children to them. The wind pierced my own macintosh and Mother's woollen cardigan which I was wearing beneath it, and I shivered convulsively. Mother had on a second-hand leather coat, which she had bought to keep her warm while doing a short spell as a door-to-door vacuum saleswoman.

Every so often I would feel faint and would start to reel, and Mother would pin me against the building's wall so that I did not fall. After waiting about half an hour, just when I felt I could endure no more, the door was opened by a probationer and the motley crowd poured in, elbowing each other in an effort to be first.

We found ourselves in a large waiting room with lines of wooden benches, and we sat down, not sure what we were supposed to do next.

I fainted against Mother's shoulder and, when I came round, I heard an angry rumbling from the waiting crowd. Apparently, Mother had asked a passing nurse for a glass of water and the girl had said coldly that it was not necessary, that I would come round quickly enough.

This indifference had riled the out-patients and they spent some time talking to each other and to Mother, in furious whispers, about other hospitals where they felt they had been treated equally uncompassionately.

We sat for a long time and nothing happened, until a nurse came and sat at a desk in front of us. Mother left me in the care of an elderly lady sitting next to her, and went to inquire when we might be seen.

'The specialist usually arrives about eleven,' the nurse said. 'You will just have to wait.'

'Could my daughter lie down somewhere?'

'Ask the patients if they will move up, so that she can lie on the bench.'

But the room was packed, so I leaned against Mother in a lethargy which passed occasionally into complete oblivion. I was so bony that it was also very painful to sit on a wooden bench for such a long time.

Finally a young physician and a nurse arrived, and began to sift through the patients, to discover their reasons for attending the hospital. Our kind neighbour held me again, while Mother went to the desk to explain our presence. By this time I was so exhausted, I did not care whether I saw a doctor or not. All I wanted to do was lie down – on the floor, if there was no other place.

'You should not have to wait much longer,' the nurse told Mother. 'Doctor arrived a few minutes ago.'

At about twelve, having left home before eight o'clock, we finally were ushered into a lofty, poorly-lit office. A thin, grey-haired man in a white coat, a man with the gentlest voice and the kindest manner I ever remember, was seated on a little stool, scribbling on a note board held across his knee. Since I had come about my throat and ears, his elderly nurse took my coat from me and sat me down in a straight-backed chair.

The doctor, a famous surgeon, smiled at Mother, when she handed him a note from our physician, opened the envelope and read the description of my illness.

He put the note down on a nearby table, and, while he looked at my face, he asked Mother a few questions about the duration of the infection. I sat with eyes cast down, hoping I would not fall off the chair.

'Well,' he said, as he picked up a torch. 'Let me have a look.'

He peered very earnestly down my throat, and then with another instrument down my ears. I winced as the ears were stretched slightly by the insertion of the cold appliance. He then felt carefully round my neck.

Mother volunteered the information that I had been subject to ear infection ever since I had had the measles at the age of five. His expression as he turned to Mother was a bit puzzled; perhaps the exquisitely enunciated words from such a battered looking woman surprised him.

He turned back to me and said gently, 'Helen, I would like to examine your chest. Nurse will take your blouse from you and help you with your underwear.'

I nodded, and unbuttoned the heavy, cotton blouse, to expose the naked, bony chest beneath. I handed the blouse to the waiting nurse.

Both doctor and nurse gasped. The doctor glanced at Mother in a puzzled way, as if to include her in their shock. I was suddenly afraid that the doctor had spotted some deadly disease.

'Nurse, bring a gown,' ordered the doctor sharply. 'I think I had better take a look at Helen generally. Help her slip off the rest of her clothes.' He looked at me and smiled. I must have appeared to him to be scared beyond measure, as I gazed at him, pop-eyed, because he said soothingly, 'There is nothing to be afraid of, my dear.'

Mother had not expected that I would have to strip, and I saw her flush slightly, as I dropped my skirt off, leaving me garbed in a pair of worn, off-white knickers held up by a pin and a pair of rayon stockings supported by rubber bands.

Almost tenderly, the nurse slipped the stiff, white gown round my shoulders, and her carefulness frightened me more.

The nurse laid me on an examination table and the specialist checked me over, part by part. I must have looked ugly to him, with only a slight rise of young breasts above ribs that stuck out, a distended stomach with a fluff of pubic hair at its base, legs that seemed all bone. I could not see my own buttocks, but I knew that there was little fat on them. He pinched me in several places very gently. Then he wrapped the gown round me, and the nurse helped me to sit up.

The specialist turned to Mother, and in a voice which indicated a rage ill-controlled, he asked her, 'Mrs Forrester, what *has* happened to this child? An illness such as your physician describes could not have reduced her weight to this extent.'

Mother said uneasily, 'She does not have a very good appetite.'

'She is half starved.' He was furiously angry, and his voice rose. 'You will lose her unless you find some means of getting food into her. No child should have to suffer like this. What is the City thinking of? Is your husband on Public Assistance?'

'No,' muttered Mother. 'He works for the Liverpool Corporation.'

'And Helen?' He turned to me, 'Have you got work, child?'

I told him the name of the organisation which employed me. The nurse had put me into a chair, and I sat staring at him, aghast.

Hunger was painful at times, but most of the time

I felt lethargic and weak. I thought I was lazy, and I was always pushing myself to complete the work I had to do.

'I can't understand it, Mrs Forrester. You are, I imagine, an educated woman, and should understand something about nutrition. Your physician *has* expressed to me his anxiety for her general condition, though he sent her to me, of course, because of the ear and throat infections. But unless she can eat more and put on some weight, she will be subject to all kinds of illness. Her ears will heal – your doctor will explain that to you. Even in this city, however, it is some time since I saw such a shocking case of malnutrition. Did your doctor recommend a special diet?'

During this diatribe Mother had stared at him with an expression of blank disbelief. Now she flared up suddenly.

'Yes,' she snapped. 'And I have done my best to give it to her – but she doesn't eat it.'

In an instinctive defence of Mother, I interjected, 'I haven't been able to eat very much, doctor. My throat hurt and so did my ears when I swallowed.'

He looked at me almost contritely, as if ashamed of his outburst, and said to the nurse, 'Take Helen into the other room – there's an easy chair there. You can help her dress in there, while I talk to Mrs Forrester.'

The nurse picked up my clothes and wrapped the white gown round me. She put a hand under my elbow to help support me as we went towards the door. At the entrance, I paused, reluctant to leave someone who cared so much that I was thin and hungry.

'Thank you, doctor,' I said, forcing back tears of weakness.

I never saw him again.

As the nurse helped to dress me and told me what a wonderful doctor my new-found friend was, an outburst of words rumbled through the closed door. I could not hear what he was saying, but when Mother joined me she was weeping unrestrainedly, and this distressed me. I took her arm, to comfort her, while the nurse said briskly, 'Doctor will be writing to your G.P. You should go to see him in a few days' time.'

Without a word, the two of us went very slowly back through the hall and out into the street to catch a tram.

'Mummy, I'm so sorry. Please don't cry. What did he say?'

No matter what battles we had fought, Mother had suffered so much herself since we arrived in Liverpool, that I could not bear to see her reduced to tears by a stranger. The careworn woman, whose arm I leaned upon, was totally different from the pretty, fashionable lady I had known as a child. I wanted passionately to erase whatever bitter words the specialist had used when speaking to her in my absence.

Mother did not answer me at first, but heaved me up the steps of a tram which arrived as we emerged from the hospital. She handed the conductor two pennies and received our tickets, before she finally spoke.

'He is going to write to our doctor,' she said finally, with a trembling sigh. 'He will make some recommendations. You have nothing to fear. You have no disease.'

And that was all the information I could extract from her.

A few days later, I managed to walk the short distance to our own doctor's house, and spent a happy hour reading all the old magazines in his waiting room, and talking in laboured German to two German patients waiting to see him. They told me such horrifying tales of what was going on in Germany under Hitler that I felt my own suffering to be very small.

The doctor checked my ears, throat and chest again. The specialist's report, he said, had been optimistic about my hearing and he hoped I would not have much hearing loss. Afterwards, he sat down at his desk, and said very earnestly, 'Helen, you must eat as much plain food as you can obtain. Don't spend your pocket money on sweets – buy an orange or an apple. Clean up your plate at meal times.' He grinned cheerfully at me.

'Yes,' I agreed. How could I tell him that I had had no sweets during the four years I had been in Liverpool, except one or two which had been given to me? How could I tell him how empty my dinner plate had been for so long?

'And I want you to go to bed early and rest as much as you can during the next few weeks.'

Rest? With so many children pestering me with their constant needs? And I was now terribly behind in night school – my only hope for a better future; I would have to catch up somehow. Then I remembered the new job – that would be easier. So I nodded agreement again.

'And during the weekends you should walk in the park whenever it is sunny, to get fresh air. Perhaps go to New Brighton sometimes and walk there – that would be nice, wouldn't it?'

Poor, benighted man. Didn't he realise that the ferry boat to New Brighton cost twopence? Princes Park was there, however, and I often took Baby Edward and Avril for walks in it. So again I agreed.

As he scribbled on his prescription pad, he said, 'I wish your Mother had come with you. I would have liked to discuss your diet in detail with her. Tell her what I have said, and come to see me again next week.' He handed me a prescription. 'Have this tonic made up and take it regularly.'

I thanked him and went out and walked slowly down the steps into Parliament Street. After such long confinement, Liverpool seemed a beautiful place in which to walk. My eyes ran appreciatively along the fine symmetry of the big terrace houses which lined the street. Father said they had been built from money gained from the slave trade with America, but they were still beautiful to me. Even the stolidness of the brick Home for Incurables seemed lighter, more cheerful, than usual. The whole district was bathed in a mid-afternoon hush, that pause which occurs in suburbia before the homeward rush from the city. The only other person I saw was a woman on her knees scrubbing the marble steps of the Rialto Cinema and Dance Hall, and I paused on the other side of the road to watch her. Perhaps, I thought wistfully, now I have a rise in pay I could go to the cinema. People said that the floor of the dance hall was a particularly good one, and I imagined myself in a long dress twirling round it in the arms of the Prince of Wales, now a troubled exile, to the strains of a Strauss waltz. It doesn't cost anything to have dreams.

Chapter thirty-three

Many years later, Alan told me that one day, while I was out, some people came from the child welfare authority and threatened to take us all into care. He cannot remember the date of this, but I think it must have been during my convalescence, perhaps while I was at the doctor's surgery. It is hardly likely that our doctor or the outraged specialist would have left such a case of malnutrition unreported. It is also possible that my astute employer may have goaded officialdom into action. Brian's skinny condition had quite likely been noted during his stay in hospital. So several complaints were probably made.

Whenever it was, my parents must have talked their way out of it. In those days, few would believe that neglect or ill-treatment of children occurred in any but working-class homes; and once my parents' original social status had been established there would be a tendency to believe anything they said. From the day on which we saw the specialist, however, Mother saw that I received the same amount of food as the other children, and it was obvious that she gave priority to the buying of food over other needs. We still did not have enough to eat, but there was an improvement. I became concerned that in an effort to feed me, she would go without herself, and this caused a reciprocal concern for each other, which improved our relationship.

As soon as I was able to stay up for most of the day, Mother began to use me as a housekeeper again, and I was dreadfully afraid that, once again, I would become the family's unpaid general factotum. I never grudged helping in the house, but I did not want to be permanently at home.

Little Edward was now nearly four and could talk well. He was a pleasant, confiding small companion, always asking questions, like Tony did. I would sit with him on my lap, his untidy brown hair against my cheek, quivering inside at the thought of being shut into a kind of slavery without any rewards.

Long before I returned to work, I had taken out my text books and begun to study again. I pressed Fiona into reading aloud to me, so that I could practise shorthand and not lose speed. This bored Fiona terribly – she hated reading anything, but she was very good-natured and, on my behalf, she stumbled through business letters from the text book and the first few chapters of *Jane Eyre*. She would put down the book after two or three minutes, during which my pencil had scampered frantically across my notebook, and would ask bewilderedly, 'How can you stand it? Why bother?'

I would smile at her and say I liked it. Embryo maiden aunts must be able to earn, I felt, though I could not have explained it to her. I did not want to end up a nervous ghost in the house of one of my siblings, caring for their children, dependent on them for the smallest need.

Sometimes, when Edward or highly strung Brian had difficulty in going to sleep, I would sing irregular French verbs or German declensions to them. Brian chuckled at the strange words, but Edward only needed a comforting hum and did not miss Little Bo Peep or her friends.

Three of the children had not been up to the bedroom to see me at all while I was ill. Fiona, Avril and Edward tumbled straight into the big double bed on the other side of the room and usually fell asleep immediately, but I had not seen Alan or Tony, and Brian only immediately before he was sent to hospital. Now I was downstairs again, they looked as if they had all grown enormously during my absence.

Brian had recovered quickly, and he and Tony had found good friends amongst neighbouring shopkeepers' children; they played in their houses or in the street. They also went to choir practices and to the church services.

Alan had made friends with one or two other office boys and clerks, and his pocket money was sufficient to enable him to go to the cinema, to boxing matches and to play cricket.

Fiona did not make many friends. Like me, she had little money. She was also very slow moving, so that getting herself to and from school, keeping her scanty clothes clean and joining in an occasional game of tag or skipping with other girls in the street practically filled her day. Occasionally, on a Saturday afternoon, Alan kindly took her to the cinema, or she beguiled Mother into giving her twopence to go by herself. Continuous performances in the cinema had just begun to be common, and she sat all through the afternoon and two evening performances, seeing the same two films offered, over and over again. She would return about eleven o'clock at night, silent and bemused. As she approached her fourteenth birthday, she began to put her hair into rag curlers and to take a deep interest in her appearance. Boys in the streets around whistled after her, and she would run into the house blushing and bewildered.

Because I had such intense pain during my menstrual periods, a pain which could not be hidden from the rest of the family because I used to scream with it, she dreaded the onset of this natural cycle, but when it came it was painless and she was much relieved. When I saw this, I asked the doctor if my pain could be at least reduced, but he laughed and told me to take a couple of aspirins, assuring me that it would go away when I was married. Through the years I got the same reply from other general practitioners.

Avril, short for her age though sturdy looking, still raged helplessly when our parents quarrelled or whenever she was in any way frustrated. Like me, her birth had been bitterly resented, and in her first years she had been left almost entirely to the care of servants. Now, however, I noticed that Mother had begun to recognise a fellow spirit, for they were surprisingly alike, and the little girl clung to her mother in a very moving way. Yet another stray cat had attached itself to our household and Avril seemed to get some comfort from cuddling it and pretending that it was a baby. It submitted very patiently to being wrapped in a piece of blanket and held upside down.

As I waited for my lethargic body to gain strength, I watched the children come and go, each intent upon his or her own business. I began to realise that life does change; nothing lasts for ever. When I had first come to Liverpool and had been plunged into sudden, frightful poverty amongst coarse and scarifying people, it seemed as if we would always be small and helpless. But it was not so; the children were growing vigorously, despite poor food.

All growing things push against each other, each fighting for air, space and sustenance, and large overcrowded families are no exception. And I observed that, as each child grew in strength, it fought quite ruthlessly for a place for itself, giving very little thought to the plight of the others. I saw that the family unit was not as tightly locked together as my parents were fond of imagining. And I was plunged into melancholy when Mother preached to me the need to go without, give up my life to the care of the children. Why could they not help, too? I would ask angrily. And the retort was always the same, 'You are the eldest.'

But, in truth, they were better at avoiding it. Alan was the eldest boy and automatically more privileged; he was my father's hope. Fiona pretended to be much more stupid than she really was, and she was more frail. Brian and Tony kept out of the way, and Avril had such a colossal temper that even Mother was silenced by it. Amongst us toddled Baby Edward, serene and self-assured, too small to have to worry.

Too sick myself to do a great deal, I sat and watched them, corrected them if they seemed to be doing anything of danger to themselves, made the meals and the fires, and wondered once if they would go hungry for my sake.

The answer, I believed, was that of Shaw's Pygmalion, 'Not bloody likely.'

Chapter thirty-four

When I returned to work, the mood of the City seemed more cheerful. The previous winter it had been hung with crape for the passing of King George V; Edward VIII, my adored Prince Charming, had come and gone, and was an exile with his Mrs Simpson. Now we all looked forward to a coronation, that of George VI and his plump little Queen, Elizabeth. It seemed also that there was a trifle more work available, though the lines of unemployed were still very long.

I said a mental 'Hello' to Minerva, looking down from the dome of the Town Hall. Belief in ancient gods never quite dies – it remains, mixed with the myths and legends of one's people, in the background of one's mind; and I believed that Minerva would help her people, if she could, and even, perhaps, an ugly little stepchild like me. It was not an active belief to be expressed in prayers; but just a cosy feeling like that given by a St Christopher medallion or the ownership of a black cat.

I was still very weak, and was thankful that I now worked most of the time on one floor of the office, though I was constantly under the subduing eye of Mr Ellis. I was allotted a wooden chair and a corner of a table on which to do my work. I became very quick at the tasks given me; and, whenever I had the chance, I would retire behind the stacks of files on the excuse of helping to put some of them away, to read, spellbound, the files' contents. They were moving stories of human suffering, sometimes covering many years, set down in unemotional prose by succeeding social workers. In some cases, I was acquainted with the family concerned, and it was interesting to see a social worker's opinion of them. I chuckled sometimes, because the priorities of the family and those of the social worker were often at odds. Most of my neighbours had the aim of surviving with as little pain and as much immediate enjoyment as they could obtain.

I learned the name of the women I had observed on the way to night school. They allowed men to play with their bodies in the same way as cows allowed a bull. Now the files told me that this was wrong; it was sinful. And I began idly to wonder about the relationship of men and women and about love. Surely there was something more to it than the conversation of the mill girls I had met on holiday had led me to think. I came across the words fornication and adultery, Bible words that I had not previously thought about. The dictionary was not very helpful.

I remembered the knowing laughter of Cristina Gomez when she had referred to Alonzo's goodness as a husband; perhaps she meant more than the fact that he gave his wages to her each week. Perhaps the wild, unearthly dreams I sometimes had were prompted by my coming into the beginning of womanhood; I blushed when I remembered them.

In my isolation from anything that most other

girls had, friends, affection, parties, dances, I had missed the usual slow discovery of sex. Whispered stories told between girl friends, the hints of it in magazines, discreet warnings and indications from mothers, had not been part of my experience. No boy had ever approached me. I had never worked out why Emile Zola's *Nana* was so wicked; all she seemed to do was stay in bed. In our early days in Liverpool I could have been raped and I would not have understood what had happened to me. Perhaps it was fortunate that I had been so dirty, so grey in looks, that I merged with the grey-black city around me and had thus walked unscathed through streets that for centuries had been very unsafe. Now, I began to knit together the romance of the many novels I had read with the facts that the files and the mill girls had brought to my attention and to understand the happiness of Cristina and her husband. The thought of the Gomez couple brought home to me that whatever physical relation there was between husband and wife it could be an enriching experience. And I imagined that lonely single men bought that experience from prostitutes.

Now that I was in the office most of the time, I came into closer contact with other members of the junior staff.

We could find no common meeting ground.

I was still grubby and untidy, though our landlord had had our house fumigated and I no longer feared passing bugs to the other girls. Even the fleas in the house had been reduced. Occasionally I caught head lice from the other children, who picked them up at school; and once I had to go to work with my head smothered in a heavy ointment to eradicate them; this caused a lot of stares and some open laughter, because my hair was pasted down against my skull, like a boy's.

Like any youngster, I wanted to be included in the girls' conversation, much of which hinged on the films they had seen, the boys they had met and the radio programmes they had heard. Though I had not been to the cinema in Liverpool and we had no radio, I had read a great number of popular novels which had been made into films, so I could analyse the plots and discuss their themes. I sometimes broke into their gossip with an observation, which was usually received with stunned silence; and the conversation would be resumed, as if I had not spoken. This made me feel hopelessly stupid and I would be quiet for some time afterwards. When I made a mistake, however, they would address me brusquely.

The first purchases I made with my increase in salary were a bar of soap and a packet of soap flakes. These were used up within a day or two by the rest of the family, but now, with a little money, I tried very hard to collect a few more clothes and to keep them clean. I hunted through the oddments table at the pawnbroker's and I saved up for a pair of shoes from Marks & Spencers.

I soon discovered that to have spare clothes was very difficult. Frequently, I came home to find the garments pawned or on Mother's or Fiona's back. This made me furious and my wicked temper would rise and for days I would be in disgrace for the outburst. I rarely borrowed from Mother and always asked specially; she had several hats and sometimes I would beg the loan of a change of headgear. I was confused. How did other girls cope with such situations? I wondered. What should I do?

And the weakness from my illness persisted, despite the slight improvement in diet. The tremendous inborn strength which had carried me through years of hardship was gone. I was wracked with pains in my legs and sometimes in other joints, and the throat still tended to acquire threatening septic spots in it. I gargled with salt and water in the hope of clearing them, but it was only partially successful.

So the strain for the first few weeks after being ill was very great, and I did not take much notice of my successor, Sylvia Poole, except to help her a little until she knew the office girl's work. I was afraid to say much to her, because I expected to be snubbed. She had eyes as blue as speedwells, which stared, with considerable perspicacity, through thick, horn-rimmed glasses. Though much shorter than the rest of the staff, she seemed uncowed by them or even by the formidable Mr Ellis.

I lived all my life in fearful apprehension, but she seemed to view life with a calm confidence. She had a firm, though light tread, and all her movements were deft and certain. I could not imagine a voluntary worker daring to complain to her that the tea was cold or that there was too much milk in it. Such complaints used to send me racing up to the kitchen in nervous haste, to fetch a fresh cup.

In the privacy of the top floor kitchen, where at

first I helped her make the tea, she asked me, 'Have you been here long, Miss Foster?'

'Forrester,' I corrected.

'Er-Forrester. How long have you been here?'

'Two years.'

'As office girl?' The blue eyes glanced sharply up at me, as she rattled cups on to saucers. The pretty red lips curved in a grimace. 'I wouldn't like to do this job for long.'

I did not know how to answer. All the underlying terror of losing my job and not being allowed to take another seemed impossible to explain to someone of her temerity.

Her smile was sweet and friendly, however, and gradually I began to relax with her. She had a very pink and white complexion and the suggestion of a double chin, which indicated plenty of good food. She had a charm, a gaiety about her which I longed to emulate.

Finally, I answered her question.

'Yes, as office girl. The job seems to offer a future, Miss Poole.'

Again she made a disdainful moue with her mouth. She was a year younger than me, but her fearlessness and her self-assurance made me feel the younger of the two of us. To my astonishment, she did not seem to think my conversation stupid; and slowly I began to talk to her about all kinds of subjects.

I had theories of history, and she patiently submitted to their being unloaded on her. I had done considerable background reading on the current political situation in Europe and I read every newspaper I could, either at home or in the library, so that, however misguided my ideas may have been, I had many of them. I had recently acquired two pen friends in Germany, who told me something of what they were being taught. Their letters were loaded with references to 'our beloved Fuehrer', and we shared surprise at anyone so monstrous being beloved. The basement waiting room held an ever-increasing number of terrified refugees from all over Europe, sent to us for aid, so we were more aware than many people of what was happening to Jewry, to trade unionists, to honest priests, under the beloved leader.

When I described to her birds that I had seen or a flower peeping up between paving stones or how lovely the Greek church looked in the early morning sun, she did not snigger. And gradually the barriers went down.

Sometimes we would walk out of the office together to catch our respective trams – walking to and from work was impossible for me at that time because I was too weak – and conversation would pour out of me in torrents. All the pent-up knowledge, ideas, theories, came flowing out, to be tried against a cool and clear intelligence. In fact, for a long time I forgot the difference between a monologue and a dialogue. When I expounded on an idea that was particularly far out, she would respond, 'But don't you think, Miss Foster. . .' and I would automatically correct her, 'Miss Forrester'. She would politely repeat, 'Miss Forrester . . . don't you think that . . .'

And my idea would begin to take a more sensible outline.

Life suddenly began to be exciting, interesting. I could hardly wait to meet her again and share another reflection with her. Every joke, every amusing incident had to be recounted.

Her parents had managed to keep her in school until she was fifteen and encouraged her to go to night school; her desire for better education was nearly as great as mine. She wittily reduced the office staff to size for me, and I ceased to be afraid of them. Her respect for my ideas added a little self-esteem to that already implanted by Emrys Hughes.

One day, she became the target for the scorn of the other girls. She arrived with her straight brown hair transformed into a soft blond, waved and curled about her face. The improvement in her looks was remarkable and I said so. But to bleach one's hair, however good the result, was simply not approved of by lower middle-class society, and the staff retired behind the stacks of files to laugh and condemn.

As she helped me sort index cards, she said with a scowl on her pretty face, 'I don't see any reason to look dowdy all my life. I'm going to make the best of myself.' And undeterred by Mr Ellis's startled looks, she added, in the days that followed, a subdued make-up to her already good complexion.

I was fascinated by the transformation.

Instead of buying soup in Woolworth's restaurant, I spent one lunch time examining the contents of their cosmetic counter, and, greatly daring, bought a tin of Snowfire foundation cream and a box of face powder. Unfortunately, when I applied them, before the broken mirror stuck in our kitchen window, they did not transform me immediately into a beauty. The washed-out, sallow complexion was made somewhat whiter and the red acne boils were a little less apparent, but the black rings around my eyes looked even blacker, as did the thick black eyebrows. However, I hopefully applied these aids to glamour again when I went to work the next day. Nobody seemed to notice any difference.

When I discussed the matter with Miss Poole, like an old granny solemnly discussing a funeral, she looked carefully at my efforts, and said, 'What about buying a lipstick and some rouge?'

This shocked me. Mother had always used both rouge and lipstick and, when she was younger, heavy eye make-up. But I remembered the servants saying that she was fast. I did not want to appear fast.

'Wouldn't it be rather – um – fast?' I asked timidly.

'Of course not,' Miss Poole assured me firmly. 'I use them. Everybody does now.'

So I went without another lunch and spent six-pence on rouge and lipstick. They were the wrong colour for me, and I did not place the rouge correctly. With my hair combed back in a bun and two feverishly red spots painted on my cheeks, I looked like a Dutch doll.

This time, Mother noticed. And she laughed at me. Cross and crestfallen, I went to wash my face.

But Fiona, much less cut off from other girls than I was, had borrowed some women's magazines which showed how to apply make-up. In exchange for a chance to paint her own face, she brought these magazines out from under her mattress and let me read them. When Mother was out, we both tried to follow the instructions, vying for peeps into the bit of mirror, as we worked. There was a special diagram showing how to place rouge on a long, thin face. I was surprised at the improvement, though the magazine confirmed that the colour was wrong for a brown haired, green-eyed person with a yellow skin.

When I looked at Fiona's more successful efforts, I realised, with a shock, that she had grown up. She laughed at my expression of astonishment. Perfect teeth flashed between the gaily painted lips. She had carefully removed, with a wet finger, the surplus powder from her huge eyelashes and smooth, long brows, and her dancing, violet eyes were greatly enhanced by the powdered skin.

'Fi, you look gorgeous,' I exclaimed.

'Do you really think so?' she asked shyly.

'Oh, yes,' I assured her.

She looked down at her grubby, little girl's clothes, and sighed. 'Thank goodness, Mummy's going to buy me some decent clothes to start work in. She's going to get a cheque so that I can have a new coat and hat and everything.'

Such a pang of jealousy went through me. I remembered the exhausting battles I had fought and was still fighting to be able to work, to have a few clothes, even to get enough to eat. Here was Fiona taking it for granted that she would have no such difficulties.

'She hasn't asked you to look after Edward until he starts school in September?'

'She knows I'm no good at that sort of thing,' she replied placidly, as she took down the mirror and tried re-arranging her straight hair in a more sophisticated style.

It was true that Fiona had always appeared very helpless, when asked to help in the house. I looked at her sharply. She had picked up the family comb and was contentedly combing her hair. I had an uneasy feeling that she was much smarter than me.

'Good for you,' I said, trying unsuccessfully to keep acidity out of my voice.

Fiona put down the comb and turned to me.

'They can afford to pay someone,' she said calmly. 'There will be five of us at work, when I start.'

'Tell that to Mother,' I snapped bitterly.

Chapter thirty-five

As promised, the Presence arranged another holiday for me. This time, I had to pay my own fare and one pound towards the cost.

'Since you will receive a month's salary before you start the holiday, there should be no difficulty about that,' she said to me very pleasantly.

I was most grateful and thanked her effusively. I nearly danced out of her office. A holiday like the one I had had before would make me strong again, take away the pains in my legs. And I could, if I wished, sleep and sleep and sleep, until my head stopped aching and my eyes lost their bloodshot hue.

Filled with excitement, I dashed into the house when I arrived home and poured out the thrilling news to my parents, who were seated at the table, bickering as usual. It took a lot of effort on the part of both Father and me to persuade Mother that she could provide the necessary one pound.

'I'll save up my fare,' I promised, as I ate a slice of bologna and several pieces of bread and margarine, followed by gulps of sweet, weak tea.

In the weeks that followed, by halfpennies and pennies, I saved the fare, two shillings for pocket money and enough to buy some stockings, knickers and a petticoat, the first petticoat I had owned in Liverpool. The day before my departure I bought the ticket, put my few clothes together in a shopping bag, and talked gaily to a silent Mother about the beauty of the Lake District.

On the Friday night I handed her my month's pay, less the rise which the Presence had quietly given to me. This latter money I had to keep for fares, stockings and soup when I returned. Mother slipped the money into her handbag, without a word.

An hour before the train was due, I asked her for a pound to pay to the Holiday Home.

'I haven't got it,' she said.

I could not believe her. But it was true.

On the previous evening, while I had been fetching some milk from the dairy, the agent who collected for the Finance Company that provided the cheques with which she purchased clothes, had called. She was, as usual, behind in her weekly payments, and he had threatened court action; so she had given him my wages. She added coolly that, since I would not now need the ticket for the train, she would like to have it, so that she could get a refund on it from the Railway Company.

I spent my holiday sulkily watching Edward, while Mother commenced a full-time job as the representative of a sweet firm. Edward would go to school in September, and she felt she could undertake regular work. I began once more to fear that she would try to keep me at home.

Within two weeks her accounts were, as she put it, in a muddle, and she was dismissed. I breathed a sigh of relief as she returned to her demonstration work in shops, and the children cheerfully ate her samples.

In an effort to improve my wardrobe, I bought two black dress lengths from the pawnbroker and a six-penny pattern from Woolworth's. I found that I could not cut the dresses out with the blunt, curved nail scissors which were all we had, so I begged a razor blade from Father and cut them out with that. It took me some weeks to hand-stitch them, but when they were finished, they fitted well; and even Mother said they looked very nice.

I had also bought from the pawnbroker a thick, brown coat. It was a nondescript garment which had suffered from being bundled up in his loft, but it was warm. And though it was summer time, I seemed to feel cold every time the wind blew, so I wore it daily.

Mother called at the office one day and asked for me. Since I was in the basement taking clients' names, Sylvia Poole asked if she could help. Mother said she wanted my coat and, in front of the other girls, a bewildered Sylvia gave it to her. I was even more bewildered, when Sylvia told me about it. And I was hurt by the gleams of amusement in the eyes of the other young staff members.

I was outraged when I returned home to find that the coat and my second, newly stitched dress were in pawn. But heated argument did not get it back, and I shivered into the autumn before I had saved enough money to redeem it.

I was again plunged into embarrassment at the office when Father sought an interview with the Presence. He wanted help to keep our many creditors off the doorstep. I am not sure what kind of a miracle he expected her to perform on his behalf, but he lost his temper and so did she. Their raised voices came clearly through the door panelling into the office in which I worked. She told him that, with five people working, his family was far better off than most.

'But there are seven children,' he spluttered defensively.

'One should not father children one cannot keep,' she retorted tartly.

The office was convulsed with laughter. Even Mr Ellis managed a subdued haw-haw, as he wrote in his big record book. I wished that the floor would open and close over me. I bent over the index cards and sorted them feverishly, while the private exit to the hall from the Presence's office was opened and slammed shut again.

Father raged, off and on, for days afterwards, and vented much of his frustration on me, as if I was responsible for my unbending employer.

I feared greatly that the Presence would lose patience with such a trying family. But she did not. On the contrary, she was particularly kind whenever she met me in the hall or on the staircase, and would stop to ask if I was well or how night school was proceeding.

A few weeks later, she was asked by the British Broadcasting Corporation if she could find someone who would give a talk on managing on a small budget. This was not an easy request to fill, because most of our clients were far from literate, and she asked me if I thought my mother could do it.

Mother was delighted. The offer meant a day trip

to Manchester, lunch provided, and a fee for the broadcast. We all encouraged her.

She spent hours writing out likely lists of expenditure, and then screwing them up and throwing them impatiently into the fire. Though she was very good at letter writing, the talk had to be written in a manner suitable for verbal delivery; and this she found extremely difficult.

I watched her struggle for several evenings, as I went about my household tasks. Then I asked her timidly if she would like me to try to write it for her. Much to my surprise, she thankfully agreed.

Since every day I read several files which gave detailed lists of family expenditures, I was able to compose a likely-sounding budget, based on Father's supposed salary plus my earnings. Then I wrote this into a chatty format and read it out, timing it by our solitary clock. It was a little short, so I added a recipe for fried herrings as a recommended standby for impecunious housewives – fishmongers nearly gave away herrings in those days.

While I stood nervously by her, Mother read it, and, with a sigh of relief, said it was excellent. I basked in her unexpected approbation.

She had a most enjoyable day in Manchester and delivered the talk without a hitch. It resulted in several complimentary letters from listeners and was reported in the *Liverpool Echo*. Because we had no radio, we could not hear her, but most of our neighbours did own radios and they were most impressed that anyone in our district could speak on it. They ceased to regard Mother as 'bloody stuck up', and

Mother found herself talking to respectful women wrapped in shawls or old overcoats, all of them anxious to discuss her wonderful budget, which actually balanced. Their questions confused her, since she had not made up the talk, and they must have been puzzled by some of her answers. The unexpected status that the talk gave her in our bedraggled community, however, helped her greatly. She was forced to communicate with our many kind neighbours and her isolation was broken. She had had to approach one or two of them before, when asking them to care for Edward, but this new relationship opened up their world and their suffering to her, and, though she often made sardonic jokes about them, she tolerated them much better.

Some of the mothers of the girls at work had heard the talk and reported it to their daughters. The daughters spent a considerable part of their lunch hours and tea breaks arguing with me that it was a pack of lies, and I found myself in the unenviable position of having to defend it as gospel truth, despite Father's request for help from the Presence. I said loftily that the debts Father had come to see the Presence about were old ones, and finally they retired to their respective gossip corners and left me once more alone. Sylvia Poole said nothing, for which I was profoundly grateful. Perhaps her mother did not hear it.

The unexpected success of my composition set a seed in the back of my mind which was to lie dormant for many years before it finally sprang to life, and flowered.

Chapter thirty-six

Pressed by youngsters who wanted to share the experiences of other children, Mother began to take us, on fine Bank Holidays, to New Brighton, a small holiday resort on the other side of the River Mersey.

Father refused to accompany us to its crowded beach, washed with the effluent of both Liverpool and Birkenhead, so Mother and I packed paper shopping bags with banana sandwiches and beer bottles filled with lemonade made from a concentrate. Down the sides we stuffed old pairs of underpants or shorts and our always dirty towels, so that the children could bathe.

We took the tram down to the Pier Head and caught the New Brighton ferry. The floating pier, pulsating gently beneath our feet, was always packed with people, anxious to spend a day away from Liverpool's heavily polluted air; and we held the children firmly by their hands lest they stray beyond the confining link fence and fall into the heaving tidal waters.

When the ferry boat's gangway slammed down, the crowd pressed forward while the passengers hurried off. Then, using prams and elbows to make a path, they charged on to the boat. Frantic voices floated out of the crowd screaming to our Aggie or our George to 'come 'ere afore you fall in.'

Pushing and jostling, we poured on to the upper

deck in search of a seat in the sun, so that we could nurse Edward and Avril. Edward invariably broke into howls of fright at the uproar and had to be comforted by having the pretty seagulls pointed out to him and the lovely shiny waves.

Then there was the excitement of watching the funnel belch smoke. One of the boys invariably got a smut in his eye, which had to be hooked out with the corner of a handkerchief or by carefully pulling down the red-edged lid.

Sweet air from the sea blew straight up the estuary, ruffling the surface of the great river. The Royal Liver Building and the Cunard Building, trademarks of the Port of Liverpool, receded, and the New Brighton tower, the lighthouse and the sturdy battery jutting into the river loomed up. The children went mad with excitement and rushed up and down the companionways and along the crowded decks, like small, wingless gulls.

At New Brighton pier, the mob poured off like black pepper out of a pot. It was a miracle that nobody fell off the gang planks into the water.

The beach always seemed to be full before we arrived, and yet, somehow, boat load after boat load of people were absorbed.

Heavy on the air were the odours of beer and fish and chips. Fathers and young men made straight for the public houses beyond the Parade, while mothers spread old blankets to mark their patch of sand. The children flew down to the water like startled seals.

Ice cream men dispensed dripping cornets, and Alan and I sometimes bought one each for the younger children, if we had money left over after paying our fares.

Occasionally, Mother sent me to a booth to buy a pot of tea – one shilling deposit on the teapot – and we drank hot tea, while the children guzzled the overly sweet lemonade straight from the bottles.

While a towel was held round the middle of each child in turn, they wriggled out of their clothes and put on the old pants we had brought with us, and then went dancing into the filthy water. It was remarkable that nobody caught any deadly disease from the sewage and chemical filled stream.

They came out shivering, splashing the water from their skinny bodies, their feet caked with a mixture of sand and mud, and stood round us while they devoured the sand-impregnated sandwiches. Then they would play tag in and out of the seated crowd. To go to the fun fair was beyond our resources, but the children were happy to be freed from constraints of traffic and narrow streets, and to be allowed to yell at the tops of their voices.

My grandmother had always forbidden me to go to the beach near her home on Bank Holidays, because it was filled with similar trippers. Nice people, I was taught, stayed at home on such days. I wondered privately what she would think of her grandchildren if she could see them.

To my mother, these trips must have seemed unbearably noisy and smelly, the people round her crude and boorish. Yet, in a way, the change did her good, too, and she always returned from them much more talkative and cheerful.

In the late afternoon, we made the long trip home, sun-reddened and weary, Edward and Avril tending to be fretful and quarrelsome, Brian and Tony still bouncing. Fiona, Alan and Avril, being very fair skinned, were usually as red as pillar boxes, and blistered by the unaccustomed strong sunlight. They groaned ruefully about it and, whenever possible, we bought a twopenny bottle of calamine lotion and sponged it over their backs and arms, while during the next few days they peeled painfully.

One August Bank Holiday, we spent the day at New Brighton in a crowd so thick that it was literally impossible by late afternoon to find a square foot of beach on which to sit. We were lucky, however, and the children stripped off and tumbled away into the water. The next day, on the front of a national newspaper, was a large close-up of the Forrester family, half undressed, with a caption describing the record-breaking crowd. Though we were not named, we were easily recognisable.

This made fuel for both Alan and I to be baited by our colleagues at work, and, as far as I was concerned, this seemed to confirm their poor opinion of me. The gulf between us widened. It made no difference, however, to my developing friendship with Sylvia Poole. Miriam, also, continued to be very kind to me, and she took me one Sunday for a hike into North Wales. I found that I did not have the strength to walk very far because my legs began to ache intolerably. We sat comfortably under a hedgerow, however, while she expounded to me the philosophy of Karl Marx and Engels. I discovered that we were both victims of The System; but her ideas seemed too radical for me to comprehend. I did learn, however, through this and many subsequent conversations, quite a lot about human beings caught in a radical belief, how the mind can be closed to argument, the path followed so narrow that even the biblical 'eye of a needle' seemed wide and liberal. I remained obstinately politically uncommitted.

Another unexpected pleasure came into my life when we discovered that the Central Hall on Renshaw Street held showings of old films. In an effort to give the poor of Liverpool an alternative to the public house, they offered a long programme for the price of twopence, and people flocked in from all over the city centre. I used to accompany Mother on any Saturday evening on which I was not giving a shorthand lesson, and it became a treat I looked forward to throughout the week, because it did not matter how shabby one looked; nobody was in a position to sneer.

Then Sylvia asked me to go for a walk with her one Sunday afternoon and to have tea with her family.

'I'll ask Mother,' I promised, rather desperately.

She seemed surprised that I had to ask permission to accept the invitation, but I could not tell her that I had been taught obedience like a peforming dog, and I rarely moved without permission.

I broached the subject to Mother, as I did the ironing on the living room table, while the rest of the family was out and Father was reading peacefully in the cold front room.

Mother was sitting by the fire with her feet up on

a poof made out of an old tin can, and she looked up quickly from the newspaper she was reading.

'What kind of a girl is she?'

Dread question. Miriam's degree had made her acceptable, but Sylvia had no such advantage.

'She's pretty – and she's clean – and she has nice clothes – her mother makes them,' I floundered, as I eased the iron round Father's second shirt; he had only two shirts, with four loose collars.

'Mm?'

'She speaks nicely.'

'Does she?'

'Yes.'

If she doesn't give me permission, I will go anyway, I silently swore to myself.

I set the iron on the fire to heat up, while Mother folded up the newspaper.

'Well, that sounds delightful,' Mother said warmly.

I stared at her, shirt cuff half folded back. Then I gasped, 'Oh, Mummy! I'm so glad you think so. I'm sure you will like her.'

Mother made a slight, disparaging gesture with one hand, as if to indicate she doubted that liking would enter into it. She had accepted the acne-pocked youths with their strong Liverpool accents who were Alan's friends, and the fact that Fiona occasionally played with rowdy local girls in the street. Tony, Brian and Avril sometimes sounded as if they had been born in the narrow street in which we lived, because remembrance of their former home had practically vanished. Perhaps Mother realised at last that we could no longer be exclusive, that she could not prevent her children adapting to their new circumstances, however unpleasant it was to her.

Now I had to approach the problem of getting a suitable dress out of pawn. Mother kept in her purse all the tickets for the many bundles of donated clothing and bedding that the pawnbroker had piled up in his loft for us.

'I could afford two or three shillings to redeem something, Mummy,' I said meekly.

'Yes,' Mother replied, a sudden razor sharpness in her voice. 'You have plenty of money.'

A year earlier such a remark would have stung me into a quarrel. Now, I was better able to keep control of myself, and I said as gently as I could, 'I'm trying very hard, Mummy, not to ask for anything, to pay for everything, so that you have one less person to worry about.'

Mother slapped down the newspaper and got up. 'You seem to be doing very well. You seem to have money for everything.' Her whole stance was unexpectedly filled with boiling resentment, as she shuffled over to the fire and poked the coals crossly.

I began to tremble at the sudden change in attitude. To gain time, I took the iron off the fire and wiped the soot off it with a piece of rag. I was clumsy and managed to sear my thumb against it. I winced, dropped the rag and popped my stinging thumb into my mouth.

I wanted to shriek at Mother that every penny spent for fares, every threepenny-bit for a bowl of soup at lunch time was painstakingly considered. I wanted to remind her bitterly that the last ninepenny pair of rayon stockings that I had bought had been taken from under my mattress and worn out by her. In consequence, I had had to appear at work with long black lines on my stockings where I had over-stitched ladder after ladder. I was still smarting from the giggles of the other girls and Mr Ellis's tart inquiry, 'Where d' yer buy stockings like them from?'

I bowed my head over the ironing again.

'Well, sometimes I do better – when I have a shorthand student.'

'Humph.'

She put down the poker and moved slowly round the room, picking up and putting into a pile odds and ends left around by the children. I looked at her back with pure hatred for a moment. Her legs were grievously lined with bulging, blue varicose veins and her shoulders were hunched like those of an old woman. Too much starch in her diet was beginning to make her fat around her waist. The anger in me gave way to pity.

Perhaps, better than all her children, I understood what had happened to Mother. I could remember her in the heyday of her beauty, when, at every function, she was surrounded by admirers. The sight of her now easily moved me to compassion. It was, however, like being compassionate towards an angry wasp.

As I began to get a grip on myself again, I wondered what she was thinking about, as she trailed around the grubby, ill-lit room.

The silence lengthened between us, till I felt the tension relax a little. Then I asked, 'Could I get my overcoat out? And the dress with the gold spots that I made?'

'I'll give you the ticket for the coat – it's in a bundle by itself. That dress is not suitable.'

'I don't know what else to wear.'

'There's a blue wool dress in one bundle. I intended to wear it for work – it came in a parcel from Mrs Walsingham some time back. You could borrow it. It fits me, so it will fit you.' She spoke in a weary, dull voice, and she did not look at me.

So the bargain was struck. I could borrow the dress once, for the price of its retrieval. I could have my coat back if I had the money to pay the pawn-broker.

I thanked her humbly.

Chapter thirty-seven

Sylvia had on a well-fitting, grey, pin-striped suit. Her golden curls peeped out from a tan-coloured sailor hat. Her immaculate shoes, gloves and handbag matched the wide-brimmed hat. The heels of her shoes gave her height, and she looked charming.

I was agonisedly aware of my old overcoat and lack of gloves. I wore the hat that Mother had had on when we arrived in Liverpool, a battered beige cloche. The coat was still badly creased from its sojourn with the pawnbroker, despite my frantic efforts with a hot iron. Underneath it, Mrs Walsingham's dress hung on my slight frame; I consoled myself with the thought that it was a very good dress, excellently cut from a soft blue wool. I had had more success in ironing it than I had had with the coat.

We walked soberly for an hour along silent Sunday streets. Occasionally, we met a young couple, dressed in Sunday clothes, strolling arm in arm, or pushing a pram with a befrilled baby in it.

Finally we arrived at a terrace house, similar to the one in which I lived. There was, however, a great difference in its aspect. The panelled front door had no dust on it; the window sills were likewise clear of dust. The front step had been swept and washed.

Sylvia took her key out of her handbag and let us both into the gloomy hall. The house smelled sweet,

I noticed, as I took off my crumpled coat and gave it to Sylvia to hang up on a peg in the hall.

She ushered me into a living room, smaller and darker than ours. It was stuffed with furniture, but its general air of cosiness reminded me of pictures on Christmas cards. All it lacked was a row of brightly coloured children's stockings hanging along the high mantel shelf, in expectation of Father Christmas's arrival. Instead, in front of the old-fashioned fireplace with its big cooking oven, stood a little, stout lady in a navy-blue dress with a tiny pattern on it. Her grey hair was combed softly back into a bun. Her complexion was rosy enough to suggest high blood pressure. Her hands were clasped in front of her, and her wedding ring was deeply imbedded in a finger swollen slightly, perhaps from years of washing with a scrubbing board. She seemed to me the epitome of all that was kind and motherly.

And mother me, she did. I was plied with tea and bread and butter and jam and home-made cake. I was warmed by the fire, and in a quiet, shy manner made to feel very welcome. I had talked without stopping to Sylvia during our walk; but now I felt shy, and Mrs Poole had to help me out with a question or two to keep the conversation going.

At one point, Mr Poole rushed in from another room. He was in shirt sleeves and waistcoat, his scant hair rumpled, his glasses slipping down his nose. How was he going to finish preparing his sermon when there was no more paper to write on? he demanded.

My presence was pointed out to him and he was

introduced hastily, but his mind was not on visitors and he shook my hand absently. As soon as more paper was produced from a drawer, he vanished immediately.

Mrs Poole told me that her husband was a lay preacher, in addition to his normal work as a city electrician. I did not know exactly what a lay preacher was, but was too shy to ask to have it explained to me. She added that there was one other member of the family, Sylvia's elder brother, who was out for the afternoon. She sighed and indicated that she was in some way worried about him. As she talked, I began to realise that I knew him.

Just before my fourteenth birthday, the Liverpool Education Committee had discovered my existence and had ordered me into school until I reached my birthday. Sylvia's brother had been a pupil in the same class as me. There were forty-five or more pupils in the class and discipline was, of a necessity, rigid. I remembered Chris Poole vividly, because he was a target for the sarcasm of every teacher who entered the room, and yet he did not seem to be particularly naughty. If there was talking on the boys' side of the room, it was invariably he who was reprimanded, though he might be one of several offenders. If a pencil was not returned to the teacher, he was the first to be checked for its disappearance. If the class fidgeted or something was noisily dropped on the floor, it was he who had to stand in front of the class as punishment. And the class was so conditioned that they took his guilt for granted, and laughed at his discomforture.

I recognised a fellow scapegoat and felt a sneaking sympathy for him.

I was never in trouble during that period of schooling. I was thankful for the orderly lessons and was happy to put in a phenomenal amount of work. But Chris, with all the exuberance of a thirteen-year old, obviously hated the inflexible confinement to a desk, hour after tedious hour.

If anything went wrong at home, it could be guaranteed that I would be the first person blamed; in the class room this happened to Chris. In Germany it was happening to the Jews. I had just begun to realise that majority groups will always find convenient scapegoats for their own shortcomings; the scapegoat is usually a small minority. In families it can be a minority of one.

So I understood Mrs Poole's general anxiety about her son better than she realised and could feel sympathetic about it. And by many small threads of congeniality a friendship grew up between Mrs Poole and me which was nearly as deep as that between her daughter and me.

I felt so enriched that I walked home from their house in a dream, feeling as if I was floating a foot off the ground.

Chapter thirty-eight

He was a short man, padded with layers of hard fat under his well-tailored grey suit, a man with a chin always blue, however well shaved. He stood silently staring at the ceiling of the lift while I took him up to the Committee Room, and I marvelled at the announcement that the Presence had that morning made regarding him. He had never spoken to me. How could such a rich man understand a very great need of the small person who politely opened and shut the lift gates for him? A need for entertainment. As he climbed the final staircase up to the Committee Room, I stared at his broad back with awed amazement.

'He's Greek,' said Dorothy disparagingly.

'He's in shipping,' Phyllis told me. 'He made a fortune.'

And I thought, very humbly, 'He's remembered how empty of fun life can be, if you have principles and no money.'

'Sylvia,' I whispered behind the files, 'He's giving us three shillings and sixpence each. The Cashier is going to give it to us.'

Sylvia's brow wrinkled up in doubtful surprise.

'It's true. It's a present to all the staff, so that we can go to the theatre. It's supposed to be the price of the very best seat anywhere. The senior staff are going to get more.'

Sylvia pushed a cardboard folder into the file, while she considered this information.

'You know, it's only sixpence to go to the Playhouse,' she said thoughtfully.

'Really?' I breathed.

'Yes. You queue up at the side of the theatre – you can't book.'

'I used to do that at home,' I said, without thinking. 'At the matinées.'

'Home?'

I giggled sheepishly, and did not answer. Liverpool was home, wasn't it?

The slip was revealing. Was I still waiting to go back home to the small southern town from which we had come? To a house now occupied by others? To a nannie who must have long since married and gone to live in the 16th-century farm house her fiancé owned?

Sylvia was waiting for an answer, another file held ready to push into the stack.

'Oh, I used to go by myself to the theatre – when I was about ten. Mother sometimes allowed me to go to the cinema if there was a suitable film – but I never went.' I laughed at the recollection, and added, 'There was a theatre in the town which had all kinds of shows – travelling ones – and I used to go there. I sat right up at the top of the topmost balcony.'

Sylvia laughed, and said she wished she had been there, too.

Mr Ellis heard the unseemly laughter, and reprimanded us. But later on I told her about Mother's lovely singing voice and how she had always belonged to amateur operatic or dramatic groups. When Brian was born and Edith had complained about the work load, Mother had formed the habit of taking me with her to rehearsals. I was a very quiet child, not much trouble to Edith. But it was a gesture on Mother's part and Edith had to be satisfied with it.

At first I sat and fidgeted in the frighteningly empty theatre and did not understand what was happening. I watched while adults walked about the stage with books in their hands and talked in loud, artificial voices. A gentleman seated in the front row sometimes shouted at them, and someone else occasionally rushed onto the stage and re-arranged the players and told them how to behave. But gradually I became fascinated as a story began to evolve in front of my eyes. There was nothing very experimental in the plays they performed and a child could understand them. Once I discovered the existence of dress rehearsals, I used to look forward to them very much. Sometimes, as I grew older, Father took me to the opening night. He always had a formal bouquet of flowers to be presented to Mother at the end of the performance, when the bows were taken; in fact, sometimes the stage looked like a garden because of the number of bouquets presented to the principals.

Father also arranged for me to go to the pantomime each year, whenever one was within reasonable journeying distance. And what pantomimes they were, filled with singing and dancing, magical illusions, uproarious Dames whose red and white striped pants always fell down below their skirts, and, of course, noble Principal Boys like Dick Whittington and lovely Princesses in silver gowns. A magic world, a paradise for children.

Since the kindly Greek had intended that his gift should be spent at the theatre, Sylvia and I decided that we would spread the money as far as it would go. By sitting 'up in the Gods', as the gallery was called, we could see seven plays at the Liverpool Playhouse.

Probably no one would have appreciated our solemn efforts more than the benevolent donor. We queued patiently, leaning against the side of the building. We always hoped to see the actors and actresses arriving at the stage door, but we never did. Instead, we were entertained by a tattered crew of mouth-organ players, concertina players, clumsy tumblers, and even an elderly tramp who would slowly put a brick down on the muddy street, lay his head on it and gradually raise his legs until he was standing on his head. He would remain poised uncertainly on the brick while a beguiling small boy ran up and down the queue with a cap held out hopefully. It was some years before Sylvia or I could afford to give him anything.

When the gallery door was opened, we would pay our sixpence and make the long, long climb up the stairs to the top of the building. Crouched on a bench, with our knees knocking the heads of the people in the next row, we waited for the curtain to rise. Coffee could be purchased at the back of the gallery, and I was torn with doubt as to whether our Greek ship-owner would mind if I spent some of his money on a cup. I finally decided that it would not be honest to do so, and sometimes I used my soup money for coffee instead. One could become very cold and wet while waiting in the queue, and if I did not warm up quickly, my treacherous throat would begin to swell and the pain in my legs intensify.

But the excitement, the magic, was a tonic to a starveling like myself. Neither Sylvia nor I realised that we were watching the early efforts of some of Britain's greatest actors and actresses, who were being nursed along by a famous director, William Armstrong. Michael Redgrave and Rachel Kempston, Geoffrey Toone and Lloyd Pearson, peopled the shabby theatre with kings and queens and princes, and I fell hopelessly in love with each handsome face, as cloaks were swept over shoulders and swords were flourished.

I told my parents I had been given tickets for the theatre. I did not dare to say that I had been given money; it would have inevitably been squeezed out of me, by reminders that there was nothing in the house for breakfast or that Baby Edward had no socks; and I would have felt so guilty that I would have handed it over like a lamb. I kept the money from my occasional teaching earnings, and the extra half-a-crown that the Presence paid me, in a bag round my neck. But often the need was so great at home that I would have to give part of it for some necessity, and go without lunch or some other small luxury. Since my illness, it had been a grim necessity to hold on to sufficient money for tram fares; it was over a year before I was strong enough to walk to and from work again.

Minerva, sitting on top of the town hall dome,

smiled particularly on the Liverpool theatres of those days, as if to encourage specially her actors to create for two young girls a world of wonder which helped to make endurable the soot-blackened city outside the theatre walls. In those precious hours in the stuffy Playhouse gallery, tucked up comfortably beside Sylvia, I was happy as I had never before been happy in Liverpool.

Thank you, dear Minerva. Thank you for all that sweet content. I knew you'd help me.

About Mama's size. Blue-green suit. Said to her family, when the Gulf war started, that if the war started, would last 10 years. Hair white with hints of greyish-black. Complexion fair with a hint of yellow. Nose wide prominent, but narrow. Thin lips, scarce eyebrows. Face oval, lower teeth still her own. Short hair, hair at neck ~~close~~ cut away. Nothing about her particularily expensive. Frame glasses. Blue-grey eyes, slightly prominent, light eyeshadowing of same color.